DIDACTIC STORIES FROM MAWLANA JALAL AL-DIN AL-RUMI

Commemorate of 800 th Birth Anniversary of
MAWLANA JALAL AL-DIN AL-RUMI

BY
ISHAK ORHAN

Rûmî YAYINLARI

DIDACTIC STORIES FROM MAWLANA JALAL AL-DIN AL-RUMI

RUMI PUBLICATIONS

44

Prepared for Publishing

ISHAK ORHAN

Preparations before Printing
Fetullah Mercan

Printing - Sebat Ofset

May - 2010

ISBN

978-605-5959-36-4

RUMI PUBLICATIONS

Mimar Muzaffer Str 42/A Konya

Tel: +90 0332 353 48 11 - 12 Fax: +90 332 352 70 90

www.kitapdunyasi.com.tr

rumiyayincilik@yahoo.com

mustafacaliskan.konya@hotmail.com

Contents

ABOUT THE AUTHOR

Ishak Orhan was born in 1960 in a small village called Yenice near Doganhisar in KONYA/TURKEY. He graduated from Yenice Primary School and then finished Middle School in Doganhisar. After then he went to Çankiri Health High School in 1974. He graduated from this school with first degree and was appointed to Konya Health Centre in 1978. At the same year he entered to Foreign Languages High School. He finished this school in 1981 and he appointed to Konya Health Job High School in 1983. In 1993 he appointed to Konya Health Education Institute as an English instructor. In 1998 he appointed to Nigde University, The faculty of Aksaray Economical and management Sciences as an English Lecturer.

He mastered at Education Curriculum and Teaching Section at Selcuk University in between 1998-2001.

He is married with two children.

PREFACE

Praise is to Allah, The Beneficent, The Merciful, who created the universe with affection and treats all creation with compassion; the most beautiful complements and prayers are to His beloved one, His last messenger and our guide of salvation, Muhammad Mustapha (pbuh) , to his family, to his friends and to the followers of the Muslim saints.

Human beings are like flowers in different colours, in many varieties...They are born like rosebuds; then they blossom with all their beauty and freshness; afterwards they wither, shrink and mix with the earth. So, their short life comes to an end. However, there are some flowers whose scents are never forgotten; on the contrary, they continue to smell sweetly. Mawlana Jalal Al-Din Al-Rumi is one of those flowers. He has dispersed the water of truthfulness and love through his works to the whole world for centuries.

Hundreds of books and maybe thousands of articles have been written about Mawlana Jalal Al-Din Al-Rumi, who is one of the highlighted characters of divine love. It seems that there will be new ones to join this cascade of writers at anytime.

The stories in this book are the bunch of flowers from him. There are the stories that teach and entertain people reading them.

Undoubtedly, because we are human beings, all of the works we have accomplished might be full of mistakes. We are in expectation that all the errors and mistakes made in this book should be attributed to us and all the beauties to Mawlana and Allah, The merciful. We hope that this work will be beneficial to all the readers.

Any effort on this way is ours and success is Allah's, the Almighty.

07/06/2007

Ishak ORHAN

MAWLANA'S WILL AND REMARKS ABOUT VISITING HIS TOMB

Mawlana made a will about the tomb that would be erected over his grave:

"Let our disciples build a high tomb which can be seen from far and wide. If anyone sees our tomb from a far distance, and believes and has confidence in our sainthood, God will put him or her among those who receive divine mercy. Especially, if he or her who visits, and prays at our tomb with full of love and sincere faith free of hypocrisy, sincere truth free of metaphor, and true knowledge free of suspicion. God will fulfil his every need and make him attain his wishes. His all religious and worldly wishes will turn out to be true."

MEVLANA'S WiLL TO HUMAN BEINGS.

I will for you;

to have a fear of God secretly and openly,

to eat less,

to sleep less,

to speak less,

to refrain from sins,

to continue fasting and praying,

to abstain always from lust,

to endure people's torment and ill- treatment,

to avoid of being with dissolute and ordinary men,

to be with kind and wise people. For, the most beneficial person is the one who does a favour for others. And the most beneficial word is the one which is short and sincere."

MEVLANA'S ADVICE TO HIS SON SULTAN VELED

"O Bahaeddin! If you want to like your enemy and your enemy to like you, then tell about him good things for forty days. He will become your friend, for there is a way going from tongue to heart as there is from heart to tongue. It is also possible to receive God's love by His great names. God, the Most High, says: "O servants, in order your heart may get a pure heart, let not yourselves refrain remembering much about me. The more pleasure you have, the more brightness of God's light in your heart you have. Just as the bread of the baker. The hotter the oven is, the hotter the bread is. If oven is cold, it does not receive bread."

THE LOVE OF THE SULTAN

One day, while the sultan was going for hunting, he saw a young girl on the main street. That young was the waitress of a house.

The sultan loved the young girl so much that he bought her by paying her price.

This fact didn't make the girl happy. The sultan couldn't know what to do under the effect of his grief. One night, he prayed by crying for the girl to recover. During that time, he fell asleep for a short time. He saw someone in his dream and he said this:

- God accepted your prayers. Tomorrow a foreigner is going to come to the palace. He is a real doctor. His remedy will cure your young girl.

The sultan started to wait for this doctor as soon as he woke up. After a while an old man came to the door of the palace. He mentioned that he wanted to see the sultan. They took the man to the presence of sultan. That man was the man himself whom the sultan saw in his dream. Shortly, he was the doctor.

They immediately took him near the girl. The doctor examined the girl. Finally, he realised that the girl had no health problem with her body. The matter was related with her heart.

The doctor who realise the fact said to the sultan:

- I need to be left alone with the patient. Let everyone go out.

The room was emptied. Doctor was alone with the patient and asked questions as: "where are you from?" "Who is there among your relatives?" "Who is close to you?" Simultaneously, he was taking her pulse.

The girl answered the questions one by one. Once the doctor eventually asked in which city she inhabited lastly pulsation of the girl altered. This city was Semerkant. Forwhy she was in love with a jeweller there. Thus, the doctor understood what the real matter with the girl was.

Later, the doctor was taken to the presence of sultan. He mentioned a little bit about the matter and said:

- We should bring this jeweller here.

The sultan met the demand. They brought the jeweller to the palace. The doctor this time said:

- Master, you should marry the girl off the jeweller. Or else she won't recover.

The sultan loved the girl so much that his only wish was the girl's recovery and being happy. Without hesitating, he did what the doctor said. He married the girl off the jeweller.

Now, the girl was together with the jeweller. She was recovering day by day. Within six months she completely regained her conscious.

The doctor, understanding the mater with the girl, this time prepared a caudle for the jeweller. With the effect of this, the jeweller became ill. He became gradually uglier and uglier. She started to dislike him.

This case broke the heart of the jeweller. He suffered from that grief and died just after a while. And the heart of the girl was full of love against the sultan. So the sultan lived a happy life.

GROCER AND HIS PARROT

Once, there was a grocer. This grocer had a parrot which had a nice-sound. The parrot was the guard of the grocer, uttered words and made fine jokes to the customer. It talked with the people as a human.

One day the owner of the grocer went to his home. He demanded the parrot to take care of the grocer.

For a while, a cat suddenly entered the grocer in order o catch the mouse it was chasing. The parrot, which was afraid of during that noise, flew from his place, escaped to one of the corners of the grocer and overthrew the rose oil bottles there. When the rose oil bottles fell down they were broken and oil in bottles was poured all around.

After a while, the owner of the grocer came from his home only to find everywhere was wet with oil. He wasn't late for realising that this case was done by the parrot. Getting very angry by this fact, he hit the animal on the head and shed it fur. The head of the parrot became bold.

The parrot whose head was bold felt numb, now he was unable to speak. The anger of the grocer went away. However, now he was in deep regret. He did his best to bring the parrot to his previous condition. He gave alms to the poor, applied for doctors, had remedies prepared.

Nevertheless, it was in vain. Poor parrot was both numb and bold.

A long period of time passed. One day, a bold man was passing in front of the grocer.

Having seen that man, the parrot began to talk.

- Oh passenger! Why are you bold? Did you break the bottles of oil roses like me?

The people present there began to laugh after these words of the parrot. They liked the illustration that the parrot had made.

THE THIRSTY MAN

Eventually, the thirsty man found a river. But there was an adobe wall, which was a barrier for him to reach the water. As he looked at water his thirst turned out to be unbearable and he was thinking how to reach the water. Meanwhile, he took a piece of adobe, which was torn out of wall, and he threw it to the water. He liked the sound of water to such extend that he began to take adobes out of the wall one by one and throw them.

A man who saw that addressed him "hey! What do you want to attain by throwing the adobes to the water continually?" The thirsty man:

- I expect two benefits of that. First: to hear the sound of water is nice as listening to an instrument to the people who are thirsty. The second: the each adobe, which I tear out of the wall and throw to the water, makes me closer to the water.

THE RABBIT'S TRICKERY GOT THE BETTER OF LION

There was a forest covered with green trees. Water used to be leaking down everywhere of it. All the animals used to live here with full of happiness.

The happiness of the animals didn't take a long time. The lion, sultan of e forests, began to upset them. Animals were entirely scared to death. Because, the lion as trapping everywhere all around and eating each of them every day. This fact made the animals anxious. None of them could walk around the forest without anxiety. Everywhere were full of traps. It was unwell to live within such a fear.

One day animals gathered under pledge of secrecy from the lion. They couldn't find a solution to this fact. After a long discussion they came to decision. And they went near the lion.

- Master, they said. Trapping all day long tires you. We also live in the fear of death. Let's do like this: One of us should come near you voluntarily. Thus, neither you deal with traps, nor we walk around the anxiety.

The lion liked this suggestion. But he had an anxiety. Would the animals keep their promise?

The orator of the animals walked one step front:

- We promise, he said. You are the sultan of us. We don't deceive you. You only sit at your court. Enjoy yourself. Each of us will come to you everyday. Then, you enjoy your meal. If you don't like it, we can send you another one. If only, don't eat our babies.

The lion was joyful.

- I don't like laziness. I like running after trap. But, I don't either want to reject you that you will keep your promise. Let's do so. But if you make treacherousness, I will kill you all. Revenge will be unfair.

Animals said:

- We promise. And they left there.

The other day, they gathered again. Forwhy there was a problem around them. Who would go to the lion tomorrow and the following day?

After a long discussion, they found a solution for it also. They decided to do this via lot whomever was chosen by lot would go near lion.

After that day, the animal chosen via lot went even if unwillingly and of course never came back.

That day, it was the turn of the rabbits. The rabbit didn't mind it.

Other animals said:

- Don't be a killjoy. Hurry up. Let us not make the lion angry. Or else, he will be unwell to each of us.

The rabbit said:

- It doesn't go like that friends. I have a plan. Give me a chance. I will play such a game that he will regret to have existed. Then, we will all live in this forest without fear. Animals wanted to learn the plan of the rabbit.

The rabbit said:

- I cannot tell, it is a secret. The secret is not mentioned. Trust me, it is the all. The rabbit succeeded to persuade his friends. It took way in order to apprehend his plan.

It was time for the lion to eat passed. He was in a deep hunger. It couldn't stand and he was mad with rage. Seeing the rabbit in front of him hours later he said:

- You, ill-mannered. How can you dare to make such a sultan wait? Why were you late?

- It is an honour for me to be your meal, master. However, something very important happened. For that reason, I was late. Allow me to tell it after that, do whatever you want.

- Tell, quickly, shouted the lion.

The rabbit began to talk by saying "master". Early in the morning I set out to come to you. There was a well-fed rabbit with me. We thought that, if whichever of us you liked, you would eat it. Meanwhile, we came across with another lion. He attacked us. Me also:

- I begged him not to touch us. We are the meal of the sultan.

Upon this, he said:

- Who is the sultan? And later he insulted you. I also, begged so much.

At least, allow me to see the face of our sultan for the last time. He said me:

- Leave the well-fed rabbit here, you may go. Tell him that, from now on I am the sultan of these places.

Having heard those words, the lion went mad. He was already very hungry, and now, there was this tactless who was insulting him. It was challenging him. Could it be possible?

- Lead me the way said him to the rabbit. Take me urgently to him.

The rabbit led the way to the lion. They set forth towards a well which the rabbit marked previously. Once they came to the well, the rabbit shuddered and moved backward.

This situation attracted the attention of the lion. And he asked:

- Why did you move backward?

- Master, said the rabbit. The lion is sitting in this well.

- Look, is he still there?

- I cannot look. Only if you hug me, I can look.

The lion commented it as the cowardice of the rabbit. He gave it a hug and bowed down towards the well.

There was an enormous lion in the water. And there was a well-fed rabbit in his arms.

In fact, what were seen were the lion himself and the rabbit? The water showed them fatter. But, the lion couldn't recognise it. He jumped in to the well as soon as leaving the rabbit.

The rabbit achieved his goal. It turned near the other animals jumping for joy.

- Happy news! He addressed. From now on, that lion won't exist. If you don't believe me you can go into the well.

Later, he told the whole story. Animals believed him. Their happy life in the forest restarted.

ALL DERVISHES HAVE IS GOD

A dervish was travelling on a ship. A pocket of gold was lost in the ship and they searched everyone. It was dervish's turn that was aware of nothing. The person whose money was lost woke the dervish and told the matter. He told that they would search him and wanted him to take his clothes off for that reason.

The dervish was so bored with that situation that he sheltered God with an entire heart and begged for God to save him.

As long as the praying of dervish was over numerous fishes emerged with a pearl in each of their mouth around the ship. But one of those pearls was worth a thousand of world pearls. The dervish threw a few pearls by taking them from the mouth of fishes in front of the man and continued his sleep with endless sincere to his God.

THE MESSAGE THE PARROT GOT

Once, there was a nice-sounded parrot of a rich merchant. The man bought it paying a huge amount of money from a seller.

After that day, the parrot became the best friend of the rich merchant. The man was very pleased with the situation. Nevertheless, it wasn't so for the parrot. Indeed, his owner cared for him well but the parrot was deprived of his freedom. It wasn't nice for him to spend his life in a cage.

One day, the merchant decided to go to India. He began to get ready for setting forth. Then the day to set forth came. He said goodbye to household. He asked all of them one by one:

- Tell me, what I shall bring for you while coming back. What do you want?

Upon these words of the merchant everyone told his requests. It was the parrot's turn. He could be considered to be among the household.

- Tell me dear bird. What shall I bring for you?

The parrot bowed his neck. Looked at man's face and said thus:

- Considering that you are going to India, it means you will see there a lot of parrots. Tell them my state and send my greetings. Explain that I missed all of them so much. Relate them that: they may fly in the sky for me, they may move around the green trees in the rose gardens also for me. The man said:

- If you want it, I will tell those to the first parrot I see.

After a long journey taking the days the merchant reached the Indian lands. He sat under a tree in order to rest for a while. Short after, a few parrots perched upon the tree. They began to sing a song.

The man listened to them for a while. While listening to them, he remembered what his own parrot told him. And he said them thus:

- Oh nice-sounded birds! My parrot sent you greetings. He said that he had missed you so much. He told that:" My siblings may fly also for me in the sky, sing songs upon the trees also for me, move around the rose gardens also for me".

One of the parrots, which heard these words, began to tremble. And short after, he lost his breath fell and died.

The merchant was upset by occasion. He regretted by the news he gave. He told personally thus:

- I think, this parrot was one of the relatives of my parrot. He couldn't put up with his longing and died.

There was nothing to do. The man went to the city. He did the shopping. He set forth in order to go to his country. He had bought everything his relatives wanted but what would he tell to his parrot? He thought upon it hopelessly.

The household welcomed him with joy. Moreover, the present brought to them delighted them so much.

The parrot said:

- Master, didn't you bring greetings to me from the parrots, with a sorrow sound... First, the merchant didn't want to tell what had happened. However, the parrot was insisting:

- Oh my dear bird, said him. I am so sorry. I told your greetings to the first parrot I saw. But one of them began to tremble after hearing your greeting, later lost his breath and died.

After hearing these words, the parrot began to tremble and he was stock-still. The merchant was very surprised and upset.

- Oh I said he. What did I do! As if it is not enough for those parrots do die, now I cause my own parrot to die. I wish my tongue were broke into two and I had never spoken.

The man took the parrot, which was stock-still thinking that it was death out of the cage. He put it to one side. The parrot, which was set free suddenly, regained his conscious and perched upon the opposite tree.

The man's bewilderment increased thoroughly. He started to mutter, "what is happening, what is this".

The parrot said:

- Master, let me tell you what happened before departing from here.

Once you told greetings and told them to fly for me in the sky, the parrot in India understood that I'm captive and he showed me a method with his that behavior. In other words, he wanted to say me to do thus. Because who will get profit from a death parrot? I did what he said and restrained from the cage. You are a good person but understand me too. I should be in the sky. I should sing my songs there. And I should live among my race. All right, take it easy.

The parrot flew after telling those words. The man stood in astonishment.

A PRESENT TO THE SULTAN

One man used to live with his wife in a cottage in a small village. He didn't have a certain job. For that reason he had difficulty in earning his life. Briefly, he was a poor man.

But neither the man nor his wife was complaining about this occasion. Working and living with their virtue was enough and much for them. They lived the day happy if they found even a piece of not fresh breaWhile they were spending such days, the mood of his wife began to change. She turned out to be complaining about their situation.

One day, she said to her husband:

- Master, what will our situation be? If we are full one day, we are hungry the other day. Let alone us... See, now we have children. They want to wear and feed well. Let's find a solution for that problem.

What could that young man do?

- Dear wife, he said. I do my best. But it is all. I can do.

The woman wasn't persuaded with those words. She said:

- I suggest you to go to the sultan, and tell our occasion. Perhaps he can help us. Everyone knows his generousness.

This idea used to come to the man's mind from time to time. But how would he go near the sultan of the sultans? It would be necessary to take at least a present while going to want something from him.

What would he take? He was a poor man.

The woman supposed her husband. A few days passed. While she was drinking water, an idea came to her mind.

- I discovered what you would take to the sultan, she said. Take him an earthenware water jug of water.

Could an earthenware water jug of water be present? The man began to laugh after hearing that. But later this suggestion appealed good to him.

- It can be, he said to his wife. Our water is good. The place the sultan lives must be a very large city. Does it have such good water? Let's see.

It was time to travel. The woman fed her most beautiful earthenware water jug with water. She sent him off giving the earthenware to his hand.

He went farther and farther, and arrived the city where the sultan had been in. Here, was really a very large city. While he was looking blankly to his around, watchmen came near him and asked what he wanted.

- I want to see the sultan, he said. The palace of the sultan welcomed everyone whether rich or poor. The watchmen took the man to the presence of sultan without making him wait.

And the sultan asked:

- Tell me, what is the matter with you?

- Poverty, the young man said. But before telling you my trouble, I want to give you the present I have brought.

- What is your present? Tell me what you have brought for me.

- An earthenware water jug of water. But the sultan and the chesses were too astonished. Forwhy up to that day, they hadn't received such a present.

- Why did you bring water?

- I had nothing to bring except water. Also, while I was coming, I walked in the desert throughout my travel. For this reason, I thought that the best present would be water.

- Well done, the sultan said. You brought us the best present. The sultan ordered to his helpers:

- Give him a purse of golden and meet his needs.

Afterwards, the sultan and his helpers drank the water.

- The water is very delicious, thank you, they said.

The young man was happy. Now, he believed exceedingly that he had brought the best present.

Then, it was time to go. The young man said good-bye to the sultan and set out. This time, he started to walk on another way. What may he see after a while? A very long river was pouring near the city.

Oh me, he said. I thought there was no water in this city. What a shameful it was to the sultan.

Then he understood everything exceedingly. The sultan liked the water in order not to make him ashamed and responded by giving a purse of golden. After releasing that fact the man said:

- It is enough for me. What shall I want more when we have such a sultan. He exists today and doesn't exist tomorrow. What is important is love and mercy.

THE HERO WITH TATTOO!

People living in Kazvin city of Iran used to have their bodies, arms and shoulders tattooed with the tip of the needle, following an old tradition and in a way not damaging them.

One day a man from Kazvin went tattooist and said:

- I want you to tattoo me without hurting me.

The tattooist:

- Tell hero, he said. What picture shall I draw?

My horoscope is Leo. Draw a roaring lion. However, draw it trying hard so that the ones who see it should be scared. Tattooist asked:

- Which part of your body shall I draw it on?

The man of Kazvin said:

- Between two of my shoulders. When the tattooist injected the pin in order to tattoo, his back began to hurt. He asked groaningly:

- Oh master, you killed me, what picture are you drawing?

- Didn't you want me to draw lion? The man of Kazvin asked:

- From which part of its body did you begin?

The tattooist answered:

- I began from its tail.

The man of Kazvin:

- Oh my friend let the tail alone. The ache of the tail made me suffer. Let the lion be without tail. I am growing worse. I am about to faint.

The tattooist injected the pain in order to point another part of the lion without considering the pains that the young man of Kazvin was feeling.

The young man from Kazvin asked:

- Which part of the lion is that?

- Its ear, the tattooist answered.

- Let it be without ear, the young man said.

When the tattooist injected the pin in to another part of his body the man from Kazvin again began to whimper. The conversation continued like this.

- Which part of the lion is this pin for?

- Its abdomen.

- Let it be without abdomen. The pain I'm suffering growing worse. Don't inject the pin deeply.

The tattooist was very astonished. Afterwards, he said by throwing the pin to the floor with anger:

- No man in the world might have experienced such an event. Who might have seen a lion without tail, without head, without ear? He expelled him from his office saying, "Even God hadn't created such a man".

WHOSE IS THE BIGGEST PORTION?

Lion, wolf and fox established friendship and went hunting. After running after animals all day long they caught an ox, a chamois and a well-fed rabbit towards evening. They dropped along the ground their hunts under a beautiful tree.

It was time to share those. The lion ordered the wolf.

- Divide those among us but equally.

The wolf said:

- My sultan! Ox Is the biggest one among those. It is suitable for you. Goat is medium size and height. Let it be mine. Let's give the rabbit to the fox.

The lion rejected this apportionment.

- Who are you? How can you dare to demand portion where I am? How can you find that courage? Didn't anyone teach you how to behave among your elders?

Later, the lion divided him into pieces by attacking with anger.

Later the lion turned to the fox and said:

- Come on, you, divide our hunts.

The fox was in fear as he saw what happened to the wolf. But he was trying not to show it.

- Master, he said. What is the meaning of dividing? You are the sultan of the sultans. You are worth everything. Now that you order so let me say: this well-fed ox is your lunch, you may eat the goat in the evening, and the rabbit is your breakfast.

The lion liked this presentation of the fox. He was delighted.

- That is the share equally. But I am curious, from whom did you learn dividing like that.

The fox showed the wolf lying on the ground turning his head and said:

- My sultan, of course, from the wolf's position.

The lion was delighted with this answer

- Well done, he said. Since you have learned how to behave among your elders, I am giving you the third of the hunts.

END OF PRIDE

A grammar scholar embarked a ship. This man was too pride of himself. He liked no one except himself.

He looked down on the shipper supposing that he was primitive and asked him like that:

- Have you ever studied grammar?

The shipper spent all his life in the seas. He only had information related with his job. He didn't need any information, which wouldn't be useful for him about his job.

- No, I didn't, he answered.

- So, said scholar. Your life was spent vainly. The shipper was hurt with that word. His heart was broken. The scholar was despising him by accusing him of being ignorant. But he didn't talk and answer anything. Then, after a while the wind made him fall into turbulence. The shipper found the opportunity he had been looking for. He addressed to the scholar:

- Do you know swimming?

The grammar scholar answered:

- I don't know. I don't have such ability.

- So, said the shipper. All your life was spent vainly. Forwhy after a little while the ship is going to gink. Let's see whether your grammar knowledge can protect you or not.

A VISIT OF A DEAF TO THE PATIENT

An understandable person who has dexterity and who can understand body language said to a deaf person:

- Your neighbour has been ill.

The deaf who heard that news said himself that:

- With that deaf ear, how can I understand what he says? What if his voice is low as he is ill? But he is my neighbour I should visit him. Then let me do thus: When I see his lips moving I can guess what he says via comparison.

I will ask him first "oh my suffering friend, how are you" of course he will reply "I'm fine" then I will say "thanks to God".

Later, I will ask "what did you eat, what did you drink". Probably he will answer, "I drunk lentil soup" then I will say "have good appetites".

Later, I will ask which doctor is coming and he will answer "this" "I will say" it is very good. He brings luck. If he comes everything is regulated.

That heavenly minded and deaf man went to visit the patient with those thoughts. After presenting his wishes to recover to his ill neighbour he asked.

- How are you my neighbour?

The patient replied:

- I feel too bad, I am about to die.

The deaf said:

- Thanks to God.

The patient became very angry about those words. He felt himself unhappy. He thought what this thank was for. So my neighbour wants me to die.

The deaf asked:

- What did you eat and drink?

With trouble and anger, the patient replied:

- Poison.

The deaf said, "have a good appetite". The patient got entirely angry. After that the deaf asked:

- Which doctor comes to cure you?

With the same anger the patient shouted:

- Azrael (angel of death) comes. But enough is enough. Get out of here.

The deaf was unaware of what he uttered and he said:

- Master, he brings luck. Be happy because he comes.

The questions that the deaf planned were over. He got out of the house delightedly as he made a visit in such a bad time and protected his neighbour's right. On the other hand he was talking to himself.

"Thanks to God. In such a bad time, I inquired my neighbour's health." He was happy to please him.

On the other side, the patient began to think.

"I supposed him as a real neighbour and a sincere fellow. He became sad thinking that he was not so actually. He began to think what he would say him as soon as he recovered.

THE FATHER OF THE IGNORENT

One day, Abu Cehil stood up in front of prophet Muhammad by concealing the piece of stones and says, "if you claim that you are a prophet, know what in my hand is, if you know I may believe you".

When our prophet says, "shall I tell what they are or shall they tell who I am?" Abu Cehil:

- So that you are so arrogant, let them say who you are.

Upon this, the stones in our prophet's palm begin to witness by saying "there is only one God and Muhammad is man and envoy of him".

Upon this, leave aside to believe, Abu Cehil throws the stones in his palm with anger and leaves the square by saying "there has never been such a master magician in that world".

THERE IS DIFFERENCE BETWEEN PAINTERS

There were painters from various countries in the palace of the sultan. Most famous ones of those painters were Turkish and Chinese.

Chinese painters continually claimed with those words:

- We are very talented. There is nobody superior to us.

Turkish painters didn't keep silence against this challenge. And they said:

- Our talent in painting is superior to yours.

The sultan wanted to give an end to those discussions. One day, he invited them and said:

- I will examine you. I want to see which of you is right about his claim.

Turkish and Chinese painters began the preparations. Turkish painters were very talented in their arts. Chinese were looking for a solution, as they knew that fact. Eventually they said:

- Our sultan, give us a peculiar room and another room for Turks.

There were two opposite rooms in the palace. They were very appropriate for that fact. They gave one of them to Chinese, the other one to Turks.

Both sides began to work. The Chinese wanted 100 varied paints from the sultan.

The sultan did his best to meet their demands. He asked to buy whatever they wanted. Turkish painters didn't want paint.

- Neither picture nor paint benefits us. We only need an object that cleans rust, they said.

Their demands were also met.

Turkish painters began to polish the wall after closing the door. They made it clean, bright and pure as the sky. Eventually, both sides finished their works. The sultan firstly entered the rooms of Chinese. Chinese were sure that what they had done will be liked. It proved to be so.

The sultan was surprised to find their grace and beauty looking at their picture. He lost his senses. There couldn't be more beautiful than it.

Later, he entered the room of Turkish painters. When the sultan came Turks lifted the curtain between two rooms. The paintings and embroideries that Chinese made in the opposite room reflected to this room's polished wall quite vividly.

The sultan saw a better and more beautiful one than what he saw in the opposite room. The paintings were so vivid and so beautiful that they were attractive. Thus, the talent of Turkish painters was proved.

CLEVER MAN

A Bedouin loaded two sacks on his camel and sat between two sacks. When going thus a man began to talk to him, asked him his country, he made him speak.

After that conversation, he asked Bedouin:

- What is there in those two sacks?

The Bedouin said, there is wheat in one of them and sand in the other one.

One the man asked, “why did you load sand to the other sack?” the Bedouin answered:

- For the wheat sack not to be alone and for the sand sack to be equal to it.

The man:

- What you do is an astonishing thing. Were not you clever enough to put half of the wheat to one sack, and the other half to another sack? Both the sacks would be lighter and the load of the camel would be lesser.

Having heard those words, the Bedouin regained his mind.

- Oh clever and free philosopher! What a good advice you gave me. But, there is something I don't understand. While you have such a good conception and such a nice point of view, how can you walk on barefoot?

Afterwards, without waiting him to reply, he wanted to have him to embark on his camel.

Turning to him again:

- Oh, nice worded philosopher. Talk about yourself. While you are so clever and thoughtful you should be either a vizier or a sultan. Tell the truth.

- I'm not any of them. I'm one of the crowds. Look at my position and clothes and understand what I am.

Bedouin said:

- You are kidding, how many camels and oxen do you have? Tell the truth.

Philosopher was bored of the questions.

- None of them. Do not ask me such questions. I'm not interested with those affairs.

Bedouin insistently:

- What are your belongings in your market? Explain them.

Philosopher answered:

- Oh, my road-mate! I told you that I didn't have such markets and prosperities.

- So let me ask your money. A clever man like you might have much money.

Philosopher answered in a tired way of all these questions.

- Oh lord of the desert! I swear I have nothing. I deal with bare food. Whoever gives a piece of bread I go near him. This knowledge and skill only gave me headache.

Upon those words Bedouin said to the philosopher:

- Walk out, be away from me. Let your curse not become entangled with me. The fact that one of my sacks is full of sand and the other is full of wheat is better than your advising and passing yourself as a scholar.

THE MAN GROWING THORN

A man planted thorn on a way everyone was passing through and running. The ones using this was began to suffer from that occasion. While they were passing through their feet bleed and their clothes were all in pieces.

They said him:

- Rip those thorns from here.

The man didn't take those requests into consideration.

- He beguiled them saying that I will do it today. The complainants of this occasion eventually lodged a complaint against the man to the governor.

The governor commanded the man to rip those thorns. The man said to the governor, "I will rip them today or tomorrow" but he didn't. And the thorns were developing roots more and more day by day.

Finally, the governor said the man:

- Hurry up! You don't know that the thorns gradually develop roots. But you get older more and more day by day and lost your straight.

Upon this warning, the man wanted to rip the thorns after a while. Nonetheless, he couldn't succeed. The governor turned out to be right. And the thorns were too rooted to rip.

The governor was an enlightened man.

- Bad tempers are also like this. If not left in time, they develop roots like thorns but you cannot rip them off from inside of you.

THE SINCERE PRAYER

One day, the prophet Moses saw a shepherd on the way. The shepherd was littering those words:

- Oh, virtuous Allah! Where are you that I may be servant of you? Let me wash your clothes. Let me offer you milk. Let me kiss your hand.

That shepherd assumed that prayer and praying God would be like this.

Upon hearing the words of the shepherd, the prophet Moses asked:

- Who are you talking to?

The shepherd answered:

- The creator of us, the creator of the world.

Moses opposed to shepherd saying that you are disrespectful to God.

The shepherd got too upset upon understanding that he was mistaken. He set forth towards to desert not knowing what to do.

Meanwhile, a warning from God came to Moses:

- Oh Moses, you departed our man from us with your words. Did you come to dose up people to us or to take them away from us? We look heart not of word. If the heart is respectful it is enough for us even if his word is not true.

Upon hearing that warning he just ran often the shepherd towards the desert. Eventually, he found him and said him:

- Pray God however you want. Don't mind my words.

The shepherd continued his way happily.

WHO ATE THE FRUIT?

The master loved Lokman most among his slaves. For that reason, the other slaves envied and looked for opportunity in order to disgrace him.

It was time of an opportunity. The slaves went to the garden in order to collect fruit and on the turning way, they ate and finished the fruit they collected and said to their masters " Lokman ate them".

The master got angry with Lokman. Lokman got very upset and said to his master:

- Oh my master! Do you want to learn who ate the fruit? Have all of us drink hot water and have us run in that smooth plain. Then, who ate the apples will be enlightened.

The master who did what Lokman said saw the other slaves vomiting while running in Jhe plain. Thus, Lokman was proved innocent and the other slaves were disgraced.

THE FRIENDSHIP OF THE BEAR

There was a big forest covered with dense trees. There lived every kind of game animals in it. Hunters who know that always came here. One of the hunters again came to the forest one day. While he was walking around the forest, an outcry was heard. It was the voice of the bear. He ran towards the voice.

What might have seen? He captured an enormous gopher snake and was trying to kill it.

The hunter felt sorry for the bear. He killed the gopher snake with his sword dividing it into two pieces. The bear was saved from the death in the last minute and it owned its life to the hunter.

When he regained his conscious, he looked at him with thankful eyes.

And later, he said like that:

- You saved my life. From now on, I won't be far away from you. I will be your servant.

The hunter didn't want that but the bear was very insistent.

He said:

- Allow me to come with you. Let me serve you. I own my life to you.

The hunter couldn't resist those insistences. And he accepted the request of the bear. They turned to the village together.

After that day everyone was speaking about the cooperation of the bear and the hunter frequently. The bear did whatever the hunter wanted as an obedient servant and didn't leave him even one minute.

The scholars of the village didn't consider that situation normally. They warned the hun-The bear cannot be a friend. You had better get rid of him.

However, the hunter got very accustomed to him. He said:

- Why not? Don't you see we are in a good cooperation? He is my obedient servant. He does whatever I want.

The scholars said him:

- All right, but this animal is famous for its silliness. The friendship of such a person is worse than its hostility.

The hunter didn't take those words into consideration. He said to himself:

- They are jealous of me. I have a strong and powerful servant. They envy me.

After a while, one day, the hunter went to the forest. He cut some wood for a while. He was now exhausted.

He lay down under a tree in order to take a rest. Then rapped, he began to sleep.

When the bear saw the hunter sleeping, he began to guard him standing by at the bedside of him. Meanwhile, a fly perched on the face of the hunter. When the bear saw that, he got agitated. Even though the bear tried to remove the fly, it didn't mind it. Whatever the bear did, it couldn't remove the fly.

It should have found another method. The only way was to kill the fly. He could only be removed it by this way. He took an enormous stone from the floor. With the aim of the killing the fly, it hit the bear on its head with his all power.

Eventually, the fly had been killed but the face of the man was divided into pieces.

THE MISTAKE OF BILAL

Bilal'i Habesi who had every nice sound and who was one the pearls of Islam used to say *HUY* for *HAY* ' in the part of "hayaalessela" while he was reciting the azan.

Some people came near our prophet and said that situation. They claimed that to recite the azan like that would be wrong and they demanded a person who recites azan to be designated.

Upon this, our prophet understood them, got angry with them and said: "for Bilal to say *HUY* is better than a hundred of HAY words and warns them not to be jealous. Besides he emphasises "or else inside you reveals you and you get ashamed".

THE DEATH OF THE FATHER

Father of a child had died. The child was crying in front of his father's coffin and was delirious with sorrow. He said:

- Daddy, where are they carrying you? They will commit you to the ground. What will you do in such a small place? There is neither a straw nor a carpet. There is neither a light nor a piece of bread. There is neither smell of meal nor a piece of cloth. There is neither a door in front of you nor a way on the roof, nor a neighbour to shelter. How will you go there?

The child whose father was dead was illustrating the grave like this, and he burst into tears.

Meanwhile, a humorous child named Cuha who was posing through with his father said to his father tuning to him:

- Daddy, I swear they carry that man to our house.

His father said:

- Don't be silly my son.

Cuha (a boy's name) answered his father:

- I think you didn't hear what the child said. What that child said are the characteristics of our house. As if he illustrates our house. In our house, there is neither a straw nor a light. Everywhere is dark. There is neither med nor garden and door of the house. Tell me daddy, is there any difference between grave and such a place.

Cuha was telling the truth. His father stopped talking and couldn't say anything.

A PROUD FLY

Once, a fly was wondered proudly and regarded itself as the king of the winged animals. One day, he found himself in a travelling ship. It was shocked and astonished. He sad to himself "oh my God! In an enormous sea, a small man directs an enormous ship, is it possible?"

When the ship approached to the shore, it flew to the earth and perched on a straw on which a donkey previously put it feet and urinated. As the straw was shaking, he realised that what he was shocked in the ship a few minutes ago was happening to him. "Why was I so shocked? Here is the sea and I am a captain of the ship". He became very proud of himself.

THE SNAKE HUNTER AND THE DRAGON

A snake hunter went to the mountains in order to catch snake. He wondered about on the mountains to catch an enormous snake in the harsh conditions.

One day, he saw quite an enormous dragon. It was dead but even with its corpse it frightened the snake hunter. Snake hunter was thinking like that. However, it was not so. It only slept by the effect of cool.

But, his fear didn't take long. He took it from its place. He carried it to Baghdad in order to show it to the public. As the dragon was rather big, he suffered much on the way.

The snake hunter brought the dragon to the cross of far ways. He wanted to make a big noise and drew attention of the public. In a short time, people of Baghdad heard about the dragon.

The snake hunter said to people of Baghdad:

- I brought you a dead dragon. But, in order to catch it I was exhausted.

The people of Baghdad informed everyone about the matter saying that, "the snake hunter brought an unprecedented dragon by killing it".

The snake hunter thought the more people watched the more money he would earn.

Eventually, the square of the city was full chock block. The curious people was standing on their finger lips and trying to see it raising their heads. Anyone wasn't aware of anything in the crowd. Everyone was together young and old, poor and rich as doomsday.

As the snake hunter was moving the carpet the crowd was raisin their heads. The dragon which frozen, was sleeping under the carpet. The snake hunter tied it with ropes against every prospect.

The snake hunter who wanted the people to gather couldn't think something. The hot and burning sun of Baghdad was shining on the dragon. The dragon, which was thought to be dead, began to move.

Having seen that situation the people were astonished. After this astonishment turned to fear, everyone began to scream. People began to run away crushing each other. During those screams, the dragon tore its ropes off. The snake hunter was merciless and couldn't run away. The dragon swallowed the snake hunter at one first go.

A REAL FRIEND

Once, there was acquaintanceship between a villager and a townsman.

The villager became the guest of the townsman and spent two or three months in the house of the townsman. The townsman met all the needs of the villager unconditionally during those visits.

One day the villager said to the townsman:

- Oh master! Do you never come to the village? Please bring your all children one day. Now, it is just spring. Or come in the fruit season in the summer. If you want, bring your relatives too. Stay three or four months.

The townsman didn't want to accept the invitation of the villager. On order get rid off he invented excuses. And he said:

"I will come later".

Years passed after this promise. Each time the villager came to town and became his guest.

He asked:

- When will you come?

Whenever the townsman was asked that question he replied:

- This year we couldn't find any opportunity, as we were too busy. I will come next year hopefully.

Insisted the villager repeated his invitation this time too:

- Oh treat! All my family waits you.

Every year, the villager visited the townsman. The townsman catered him and took him under his protection. Eventually, the generous townsman entertained him for three months. After those honouring the villager said to townsman.

- I thought you would come and be my guest. You always deceive me. This time, I want you to swear concerning your coming and he made him to swear.

Ten years passed. Each year the villager invited the townsman with different appeals, promises and oaths.

One day, children of the townsman said him:

- Daddy, you worked hard for the villager. You did your best for him. He wants you to be his guest too. So he can fulfil his dues. He requested us to take you to the village. Let's go now.

He said to his children:

- You are right but they say "avoid from the misdoing of when you made favour." Friendship is at final breath. I'm afraid that our friendship with the villager will end.

The every lasting invitations of the villager put him into a difficult position. One the other hand his children were insisting. They said:

- Daddy, if we go to the village we can walk around and play.

The townsman again invented various excuses. But, he couldn't resist the insistences and decided to go to the village. They began to prepare. After they completed preparations, they set forth getting on the donkeys. In the daytime, their face was too hot due to sun at night; they learned how to find way via moon.

Now the village was seen but it was not the villager's. He turned to another way. They walked around different villages during one month. Forwhy they didn't know the village, which they would go.

Then, they were fed up with villages and villagers. After one month, they reached the village in a very hungry position.

The guests found the house of the villager by asking and ran to the door as if their relatives. Bt the ones inside didn't open the doors. The townsman was very upset because of this behaviour and he became too angry.

In the black frost of the night, under the hot rays of the sun in the daytime, they stayed in front of the door five days and five nights. The townsman greeted the villager whenever he was and told who was. But the villager pretended not to know him. When he said:

- "May be you are telling the truth but, how can I know whom you are and if you are an honest man or not", he was astounded. He asked:

- How can you say such a thing? Didn't you eat on my table and be my guest for months?

The villager answered:

- Do not talk nonsense. I neither know you nor your name and place.

Days passed like this. In the fifth night the clouds covered the sky. It began to rain cats and dogs. By the effect of rain, the townsman reached his limit of endurance. He came to the door of the villager. He began to knock it. After thousands of insistences, the villager came to the door. He asked:

- What do you want a curse of God? The townsman was very angry.

- I renounced my old rights. I gave up the goodness I though I had done for you. Now, show a place to shelter in this rainy weather so that you can do a good deed. See that my family was bewildered.

The villager answered:

- It's okay. There is a small shed there. The gardener waits and guards there. If you do the same work and endure the difficulty, let it be yours.

The townsman answered:

- I serve you. At least, show me a place. I don't sleep, I guard for the grapes. If the wolf comes I will kill it.

Thus, he sheltered the shed at the night when it was raining cats and dogs. They tried to sleep in the shed piling up each other. On the other hand they said:

- Oh God is it justice to us?

Although the townsman had arrows and bow in his hand, he guarded the garden all night long and he was taking measures for it. He protected all around for the wolf not to give harm. One the other hand, in the shed mosquitoes and fleas beat the children as if a wolf.

Thus, it was middle of night. Suddenly, there appeared a shadow of wolf on the hill. The townsman threw an arrow and killed the animal. While the animal was falling down it forted, having heard that noise the villager said:

- Oh bad man, what you shot is the foal of my donkey.

The townsman said:

- No, it is a wolf. Look at his shadow; it is obvious that it is a wolf.

The villager said:

- No, I recognize the foal of my donkey with the voice of its fart. I distinguish it as I distinguish water from sweet drink. You killed my food walking around my garden. Do not live in happiness.

The townsman said:

- Look well, now its night time. One cannot see well at night. I recognize it. I distinguish its foot.

The townsman couldn't endure, stood up and buttonholed him and said him:

- Oh trickster stupid! I think you are drunk. Now that you can distinguish your foot by its foot, how cannot you distinguish your four years as friend?

DOES NOT LEAVE OUTSIDE

One day, a man wanted to go to a Turkish bath. In the early morning, he called his servant.

- Sungur! Wake up now! Take the cup and loin-cloth; let's go to Turkish bath.

Sungur set forth with his foster after completing required preparations.

There was a small mosque on the way. Sungur heard a nice azan sound. He was keen on performing the ritual prayer. He said to his master.

- Master! Sit a while in this market, let me go and perform my ritual prayer.

Master said "all right".

Sungur went to small mosque with pleasure. He performed his ritual prayer with community. It was prayed. Both community and imam got out of the mosque.

Sungur stayed a long time in the mosque. The master was waiting him outside.

Upon seeing Sungur was late the master couldn't endure. She called him out.

- Oh Sungur! Why don't you get out?

Sungur replied:

- Oh master, he doesn't allow me. Be patient. I will just come. I haven't forgotten you.

The master continued waiting. Time was passing but Sungur was not coming. Upon that, he shouted to Sungur saying, "come" for seven times.

Eventually, Sungur was fed up with that behaviour of the master. And he said:

- Oh my respected master, he doesn't allow me.

The master asked in an astonished way.

There is nobody in the small mosque. Who doesn't leave you?

Sungur answered like this -Who compelled you outside, compelled me inside. Who doesn't allow you to the mosque keeps me inside, doesn't allow outside.

THE ELEPHANT

Indians brought an elephant in order to show the people and captured it to a dark stall. In order to see the elephant many people gathered in front of the dark stall. But, the stall was so dark that it was impossible too see the elephant.

For that reason, in order to understand what was inside, everyone was touching the elephant and trying to define it in this way. One of them thought the elephant's trunk. This man said:

- Elephant is like a grove.

Another one thought elephant's ear. He said:

- I think it is a fan.

Another one thought its foot. He said:

- I think it is like a column.

Another one thought its back. He said:

- The elephant is like a throne.

Thus, everyone thought somewhere of the elephant, whenever they thought, they began to express It by defining what they thought.

None of their definition was some with others'.

THE SCORPION AND THE FROG

It was a spring morning. A frog was sunbathing by itself in the riverside. After a while, a scorpion got out of the bushes. It greeted the frog with a fake smile.

- Good morning brother, what a nice day, isn't it? Hearing the voice of scorpion spoilt the frog's good mood. Forwhy there was no trust to the friendship of the scorpion. For that reason, it didn't take it into consideration. The scorpion was insistent. It pretended sincerely and said:

- I think you didn't hear me. I greeted you friendly.

The frog said:

- You cannot be a real friend.

The scorpion said whimpering:

- Do you think so too? Everyone knows me wrong, I am a good scorpion, I want to establish a friendship with you. Moreover, now I need you. Please help me.

The frog couldn't resist upon hearing "help" word. It asked:

- What do you want?

- Would you please cross me the river by carrying me on your back?

- All right, how will I trust you? What if you harm me?

- Can it be? Badness cannot be return of badness.

The frog couldn't resist. It was good- hearted. It said:

- All right! Get on my back.

The scorpion got on frog's bag. They succeeded crossing the river by swimming. They came to the opposite side. Just as they were embarking on earth, the scorpion thrust the poisonous pin. Poor frog said with acute pain.

- What did you do? Would you reply my goodness like this? I thought you had promised.

The scorpion said:

- What shall I do? This is my old habit. I cannot give up.

While it was giving its last breath, the scorpion said to the frog:

- You are right! There must be no trust to a bad one. Let my condition be an example to everyone.

QUARRREL FOR GRAPE

Four men whose languages were different were friends. One of them was from Iran, another was Romanian, another was Arabian and the other was Turk. These for friends were walking around together. They had no money. One man gave them some money and he said:

- Buy whatever you want with this money.

The man from Iran said:

- Let's buy "engur" with that money. The Arabian objected:

- I don't want "engur". Let's buy "ineb". Turk said:

- No I don't want "ineb". I want "uzum". The Romanian said:

- Let alone those words. Let's buy "istafil" with that money.

Thus, these four friends began to quarrel. Because, they weren't aware what each of them wanted.

While they were discussing what they would buy, a man who knows those four languages came near them. He witnessed the quarrel of those four friends. He asked:

- What are you doing, what is the reason for this quarrel?

One of them explained the situation. The man said them:

- Oh, stupid men, already all of you are talking about the same thing: "engur" means in Persian language "grape", in Arab language, "istafil" in Roma language means same thing. Why do you quarrel all of you want the same thing

SINCERE PRAY

A man was the guest of a blind man. His curiosity rose up when he saw an opened Koran on the table. The man was blind but Koran was opened.

He went to bed with that idea and in that curiosity but he could not sleep however, he began to wait in the bed.

The landowner woke up after midnight. After performing ablution he sat in front of Koran and began to read. He was reading so well that the guest couldn't stand. He stood up and went near the man. He saw that the man was following the lines with his finger. He couldn't conceal his astonishment and he decided to ask how that could happen.

The landowner "there is nothing to be surprised. Before my eyes became blind I used to read Koran but it was not in my memory. But I loved too much. I beg to God. I prayed him to open my eyes while reading Koran and he accepted. There is no difficulty for God as long as we know how to want" said.

THE OLD PATIENT

An old man didn't feel himself well. For that reason, he went to the doctor.

- I am confused, my mind is not all and my conception is in utter disorder.

Doctor replied:

- This confusion is result from old age.

The old man was not satisfied with this answer. He asked again:

- I cease the value, I cannot see clearly.

- It is resulting from old age, too.

The patient continued his complaining:

- My back aches too.

The doctor said patiently, turning to the patient:

- From old age, from old age.

The patient went on complaining.

- Whatever I eat, I cannot digest. I have trouble when breathing. Is it resulting from old age too?

- Yes, it is. Already when you get old, you have thousands of problems.

The patient got angry and said:

- What kind of doctor you are! Is that all you can do? Did you learn this in medicine? You don't know that God gives the cure of every illness.

Doctor finally said those words calmly.

- Oh, old man! Your anger is result from old age too.

END OF PRESUMPTUOUSNESS

A small mouse was going proudly by taking the halter of a camel in his hand. The camel felt no disturbance in accompanying the mouse, as it was benign creation. The mouse said secretly:

- How brave I am! I drag an enormous camel after me.

The camel understood this idea of the mouse. It said secretly:

- Comfort yourself, I will show you soon. They gradually came to the shore of a big river. It was such a big and deep river that even an enormous elephant couldn't pass it. The mouse stop there, it was astonished and petrified.

The camel found the opportunity it was looking for. It said to the mouse:

- Oh, my accompaniment everywhere! Why did you stop! Now cross the river bravely. Aren't you my guide and vanguard? Don't stop in the middle of the way. The mouse said:

- My friend, the water is too deep. I am afraid of to be drowned.

The camel said in mocking way: -Let's see what the dept of the water is. And stepped to the river and later said:

- Oh, blind mouse! Water is the knee- deep. Why were you surprised?

The mouse said:

- Oh, skilful camel! It is knee-deep for you but it is a hundred cubits over me. The camel said:

- So, be moderate for the next time. Don't behave insolently. Go and challenge with mice like yourself. You cannot compete with meThe camel felt pity for mouse.

- Come on! Get on my back. It is my due to cross that river. I can cross hundreds like you and they crossed together.

THE IMPORTANCE OF MENTAL ABILITY

They were three close fishes before they used to live alone. Later they were bored and they decided to establish friendship.

After that day, those three fishes began to spend time by playing various games until evening meeting by meeting in the same place every morning. Three of them were happy with this company.

The first fish was very clever. He used to feel every danger before and took required measures. The second one was half-minded. But as it wasn't utterly deprived of its mind, he used to find solutions for himself. It used to entertain its friend inventing various games. The third one was a full stupid. More over, he was also lazy.

It was a day they were playing game together. Fishermen came to lakeshore in order to catch fish. While they were looking lake, they saw those three friends of fishes. They became happy thinking that their lot for that day was there.

The fishes were not aware of the fishermen yet. They were playing finely. One of the hunters couldn't kill them. He said to his friends.

- Those must be the three famous fishes. Let's not kill them.

His friends objected, they said:

- If cannot be, we cannot miss this lot. Also the fishes are to be caught. No one can deprive us of that pleasure.

While they were discussing, three fishes, which sensed the danger, quieted their games. They should have found a solution for that problem.

One of them was the cleverest of all, it said:

- Friends, we are face to face with a danger. We should immediately leave that lake. If we swim quickly we can reach the sea and be saved.

The other two fishes objected this idea. They said:

- Here is our civilisation. If you want you can go. We won't leave.

The first fish, which understood the level of the danger, greeted its friends and began to swim towards the sea.

The second fish was half-minded. Even if it was late, it understood the level of the danger, it said:

- Now that we are not going, let's pretend to be dead. None of the fishermen catches a dead fish.

The third fish didn't accept this idea, either. It said:

- You do so. I will continue playing. Perhaps, the fishermen will go. It didn't take the danger into consideration.

The second fish took the measure it had thought. By preventing to be dead, he stayed motionless on the surface of the water. It was being drowned by the current; it was waiting as if not breathing. Meanwhile the fishermen prepare their nets in order to throw them to the lake. They saw that one of the fishes disappeared, the other one died. Thinking their lot was that, they threw their net in order to catch the third fish.

The third fish understood the danger upon seeing the net, but it was too late. Even if it wanted, it could not escape now. Although it tried its best not to be caught, it couldn't succeed.

While it was waiting the minute it would be cooked, it was saying to itself:

- What did I do? Why didn't I take measure although I realised the coming danger? I was absorbed in game and lost my consciousness. If I come to the world once more, I won't do this any more. I will be alert in case of danger and take measure. But, helplessly those words couldn't rescue him from being food of fishermen.

THE PEACOCK

A peacock was plucking its feathers with its own beak. A philosopher was walking around there. When he saw that the peacock was plucking its feathers with its beak, he surprisingly said:

- Oh, peacock! Why do you pluck such beautiful feathers? It is such extend that people who reads books regard them beautiful and out them in their books. People who want to cool themselves in hot weathers do fan with your wings.

The philosopher was trying to dissuade the peacock from what it was doing. It was continually plucking its feather not taking into consideration what the philosopher said.

The philosopher got its indifference and said:

- Oh, peacock! Don't pluck your wing. Don't make disrespect to make that beautiful face resembling morning sun worse. Come on and give it up.

By the effect of those words, the peacock began to sob. It cried so long and so helplessly that whoever there were, began o cry.

The philosopher who asked, "why are you plucking your wings" was unanswered. He regretted to have asked. He began to cry too. It was saying secretly that:

- Why did I ask vainly. The peacock is too sorrowful and grieved. I added sorrow to its sadness with my question.

There were a hundred of answers in the tears dropping from peacock's eyes. When it stopped crying:

- Oh, brother! Forwhy you have been deceived by the smell and colour. Cannot you see philosopher because of those wings I suffer much? Many people who are keen on these wings try to hunt me by trapping. The archers try to kill me by throwing their arrows. How can I get rid them of? I can do it by going an ugly and irritating appearance. That is what I am doing.

THE STORY OF THE HUNGRY DOG

A man had a dog, which he loved much. One day it became ill. It was about to die.

He was crying for that and burst into tears. On the other hand, he said:

- Oh, my greet troubles!

A beggar passing through there meanwhile said upon seeing the situation:

- Why are you crying? Why are you wailing?

The man answered:

- My poor dog is going to die in the middle of the road. How don't I cry? My poor dog used to hunt for me in the daytime and guard me at night. It was such a skilful helper that, it saw everything immediately with its sharp eyes. It used to catch its chase immediately, run after the thief. Oh my poor dog!

The beggar was a curio while the owner the dog was moaning and enumerating its skills and he asked:

- So, what happened, did it become ill or was it wounded?

- No, none of them. It is because of hunger. It got thinner, it was wasted away, and he answered.

- The beggar was astonished. He looked at the dog in the man's bag. Turning him, he asked:

- Oh, man! What is there in your bag?

- My bread and food remaining over last night, when I am hungry I eat them.

The beggar said:

- Why don't you give food to the dog?

The owner of the dog answered:

- I am not so merciful. There is no bread without money but to cry is tree.

The beggar was very surprised, he said with anger:

- Oh, stupid man! What a pity for you. As for you, the bread is with you and crying is free. Due to this, you watch the death of your dog.

The beggar went away by cursing him.

THE REAL LOVE

They were on the way for days. They were very hungry. Their food was already finished. For some time they were thrifty with the fruit of the trees they saw, but they wanted to eat bread.

There was a shadow far away. All of them began to wait with excitement. Sooner, the man who came near them was an old man with white hair. It was as if he was coming from far to. After greetings, they started talking:

- Where are you coming from grandfather?

- Too far, from India.

The youth having heard that said:

- We are going there too, but we have never been in India. Would you please tell us about there?

The old man answered:

- Of course and he began to tell. It is a very beautiful country. It is like paradise. It has various kinds of animals and trees. Moreover her elephants are worth seeing.

The young passengers hadn't heard anything of elephants by that day. They began to ask questions about it:

- Can we get on the elephant?

- How powerful are the elephants?

The old man told all he knew about the elephants. One of the passengers who was hungry asked:

- Is the meat of the elephant delightful?

The old man smiled. When he realised that the passengers were hungry, he gave the bread in his bag to them. While they in a trice ate the bread, the old man said those about elephant's meat:

- Especially, the meat of baby elephants is very delightful. But, do not tend to kill a baby elephant. Forwhy mother elephants are too rancorous. It tries its best, finds you and takes its revenge.

The young said:

- All right, we won't forget what you said.

After greeting the old man, they continued their way. The old man was not satisfied yet. Again, they began to look for food. Meanwhile, they saw a well-fed baby elephant, which was trying to drink water by the river.

They looked each other. They were hungry but what the old man said was still in their minds. Later, their hunger was superior. They looked bought right and left. The baby elephant was alone. There wasn't its mother. They decided to catch the baby and cut it.

Their youngest one said:

- What are you doing? What did the old man say us?

But they weren't well enough to hear those words. They rebuked their youngest brother. They said:

- Will we believe that what the old man said!

The youngest one said:

- I won't join you. Do whatever you want. I can only warn you.

The rest seven boys attacked the baby elephant as grasping wolves. After a short struggle, they caught it. They set fire after collecting some woods. They divided the skin of the animal from it's body. They began to taste its meat.

The youngest brother was anxious about the end of this act. He stayed away from them against all possibilities.

Meanwhile, the meat was cooked. Everywhere was full with the smell of meat. They began to eat it with an appetite. Even though they invited their youngest brother, he didn't mind their invitation.

Now, they were satisfied. They drank water from the river. They began to sleep lying under a tree.

The youngest one didn't sleep. His boredom gradually rose. After a while, he heard a scream from the depth of the forest. This was the voice of the mother elephant. It came near the river with a high speed. There were only the bones of its baby. It kissed and smelled them. It burst into tears. It went to the sleeping ones with hatred. It smelled their mouths. After making it clears that they were the killers of its baby. It cheated them one by one. It riddled them with its sharp teeth.

It returned near the bones of its baby. I kissed and smelled them once more. It began to cry again.

After a while it seemed to calm down. It came near a tree, which was shivering. The youngest brother was whimpering but the elephant was calm. It kneeled in front of the boy. It looked at him with wet eyes. It was as if it was pointing out the boy to get on his back.

When he realised, he got on its back by patting the elephant's trunk with love.

As soon as the boy got on its back the elephant popped. It began to run with a very high speed. Without resting, it passed mountains, hills and rivers. It took down the young boy near a big city.

While the elephant was living the young boy, it kissed him by elongating its trunk. Same as it was kissing its baby. It was as if thanking him for he hadn't eaten its baby.

The young boy came to the city after separating from the elephant. He told what he had experienced to the soldiers waiting in front of the city. The event was unbelievable. The place where the elephant took the boy was too far. That is to say, the elephant felt obligation to him as hi didn't misbehave its baby and brought him by here.

When the young boy found his way, he thanked God. He told thought that he owned much to God who gave him patience and who protects him from trickery.

THE END OF FORGERY

The young jackal wasn't pleasant with its situation. He found himself ugly. Especially, when he saw its own image on the water after it came the river shore he hated himself. He used to say on such occasions:

- Oh, my God! Why did you create me so ugly? I wish you hadn't created me as a jackal.

Who was thinking that was actually himself? The other jackals weren't thinking like him. They were angry with him as he told like that. Especially, his grandfather used to say him:

- My son! Don't think like that. Would it be better if you had been created as an earthworm?

But, it was in vain. The young jackal didn't listen to the words of his grandfather.

In fact, the result for him to regard himself like that was the behaviour of other animals. Especially monkeys were kidding him.

It could not go on like that. Some one regarding him inferior could not live in community.

Thus, it decided to run away from its nest. Would it explain it to its family? It hesitated for a while. It would be better to tell. He said:

- I will go far away.

Its mother began to cry in a sorrow. But, it couldn't persuade its baby not to go. The insistences of its father and grandfather were in vain. It would go from there.

Even without saying "good bye" to its family it set forth. But, where would it go? What if they would kid it where it went?

It was the best to go from desolate ways. Thus, no one would see him. He went and went. He was too hungry. There seemed a village at the distance. When it became night it would go there, steal a chicken and would satisfy itself.

It was evening. Everywhere was dark. He came to the city thinking that it was the right time. All were sleeping. But it didn't smell chicken smell. Perhaps, it would go to a market and find something to eat. Time didn't pass much and it saw a market whose windows were left open. He immediately went in.

What was that? He couldn't see in front of him, his food hanged to the moulding of the window, and he rolled by loosing its bounce.

This wasn't the all. He fell into a dyer's vast. He could get out of it with a great effort. There was nothing to eat in the market.

It found the window with great difficulty and got out. It turned to the forest. Now cold was added to the hunger. It began to regret having left it family and it home. It said:

- I wish I were sitting in my warm house. I had listened to my elders.

Having been exhausted, hungry and cold he fell asleep. In the following morning, he woke up with the hot lights of sun. Now, he felt hungrier. He thought he would take a shower in the river, and then look for the meal.

It came to the river shore. As usual, he began to watch himself in the water. What would he see?

Its appearance in the water wasn't as before. All parts of his body were covered with points. It liked that appearance. It gave up having a shower and watched itself with admiration. It said:

- Oh me! Now, I am something good. Now if peacock sees me it will envy me.

He wanted everyone to see him. Let's see what they would say now. Of course, they will envy it smartness. It began to walk towards it home forgetting even it hunger.

The animals, which saw it while going, were very surprised. Who was that creature? They had never seen such a creator.

The jackal continued it way without minding them. It interpreted their glance as a sign of envy.

It came around it home. It was very excited. What would it mother, father, grandmother and especially it jackal brothers say? How would they welcome it?

The baby jackals were playing near it home. They began to scream with fear. Having heard their noise all the animals there got out. What was happening?

It was a strange creature. They were about to identity it but what was the problem with it colour. The jackal was staring them pleasant with it situation.

Later, with the noise, it family got out of their home too. First, his grandfather saw him. He wasn't late to identify him. He said:

- You, you are my proud grandson. Tell me, what happened.

- I became more beautiful said the young jackal. Now, you can be proud of me. I am the most beautiful jackal of here. Moreover, I am a peacock not a jackal. Yes, I am so; don't call me "jackal" any more.

This was denial of one's own identity. All of them were angry. Especially, it grandfather and he said:

- So that you are a peacock, what are you doing here? Peacocks walk around in the rose gardens. Moreover, they do it with a swaying movement. Now, sway so that we can see what kind of peacock you are.

The jackal hadn't thought of that yet. It said:

- I cannot do.

His grandfather said:

- Then, crow. Because peacocks crow.

- I cannot do it, either.

The old jackal said:

- Can you see. As if my grandchild looks down on us, it also denies it identity. It says it is not a jackal. It is necessary to punish such a person. I reject him to. Come on! Get it out!

Already the other jackals were furious. They threw it out of the town by hitting with whatever they grasped, stone or stick.

The young jackal was again alone. He was very regretful what he had done. He immediately jumped to the river. He cleaned the points from his body. On the clean water he looked at himself. He was again as before. But, now he didn't find himself ugly. He regained his consciousness. He came back to his village. He excused from everyone. He wanted them to forgive him. He said:

- I am not a peacock, I am a jackal. I am one of you and I am proud of this.

His grandfather embarrassed him. The people of the village also forgave it. After that day, the young jackal didn't make such mistakes.

THE EXAMINATION

Sultan of a country bought two slaves in order to make them work in his court. He called one of them out and began to talk to him. Sultan wanted to learn the tempers, intelligence and skills of the servant he bought.

Sultan found the first slave he spoke understandable, clever and humorous. The slave was giving such answers to sultan's questions that another one could give those answers after thinking five hundred years. It was as if there was a knowledge sea inside of him. This sea was full of word pearls from the beginning to the end. When sultan regarded that slave intelligent, he left him.

Later Sultan called the other slave

The second slave came to the presence of sultan. His mouth was bad smiling. His teeth were also black.

The sultan didn't like his speech. However, he still wasn't able to refrain from learning the secrets and researching the unknown occasion of him. The sultan said to him:

- Stay away from me with appearance and ugly smiled mouth but don't go far away.

And he added:

- Sit there and tell some stories so that I can understand your level of mind.

Turning to the slave that he talked to previously, sultan said:

- That is your turn! Go to Turkish bath and take a good shower.

After the other one had left he said to the salve that he had wanted to make speak.

- You are a smart person. Actually you are not a slave. Your friend hat had spoke before you uttered bad words for you. I see that you are not such a person as he mentioned. Your friend said that you were a thief and not an honest man.

The slave said:

- He always tells the truth, I have never met such an honest person like him. Whatever he says is right. My master! Perhaps, he has found lots of vices of me. But, I cannot see that vices of me.

Sultan said:

- Come on! As he told your vices, tell his vices, too. So we can realize the truth.

The slave said to sultan.

- My sultan! He is really a good friend of mine. But, let me tell his vices .His vice is love, loyalty and humanity. His vice is intelligence, honesty, and friendship. Another vice of him is modesty.

Sultan said:

- Do not exaggerate while praising your friend. While you praise him, you also praise yourself. I can examine him so that you get ashamed.

The slave said:

- No, my sultan! I have never praised him.

The sultan said interrupting him:

- Let alone praising others. Mention about yourself. What do you have? What did you earn? Which pearl did you take out from the sea of life?

This speech became longer and longer. After a while, the other slave came from Turkish bath. Sultan invited him to the presence of him. Said to him:

- Good health to you. You became so nice, so beautiful. But, it would be better if you didn't have the vices that your friend told. Then who sees you would be happy.

The slave said with a voice full of anger and excitement:

- My sultan! Tell me a little of the words that stupid told about me please.

The sultan said:

- First, he told your hypocrisy he said you were good tempered in appearance but actually you were bad tempered.

The slave got very angry after hearing the bad words that his friend uttered about him. He became extremely angry and he was enraged. His face became red. He said the sultan-Before, he was my friend but he was foul-mouthed. He almost ate dirt as a dog in scarcity.

Sultan who realised the slave who was looking forward to speaking in order to gossip about his friend, said to him:

- That is enough. I examined but at with this trial, I understood that your soul is ruined and his mouth smiles ugly. From now on, you will fallow his orders. And your friend will be your superior. You will do everything he orders.

HOW CAN THE SNAKE IN THE STOMACH BE OUT?

A clever man got on his horse and was going. Meanwhile, a snake was about to enter to the mouth of a man who was sleeping under a tree. After seeing that situation the horseman began to run with his horse in order to frighten the snake. But, he wasn't successful. The snake was already in the stomach of the man.

The horseman was a clever man. He hit the sleeping man with knob twice or three times.

The man woke up with the pain the knob caused, he ran away under a tree. There were many rotten apples under the tree.

The horseman said:

- Oh pained man. Eat those apples or else I will beat you.

The man said:

- Oh, master! What did I do that you torture me? What is the reason for that? What an inauspicious man you are. Where did you come from?

The man to whose stomach the snake entered was continually cursing the horseman and heaping curses on him. The horseman said by not minding all of them:

- Eat, or else I am not responsible for you.

The man ate the rotten apples with the life fear. And later, the horseman said him:

- Now, run in that plain. He began to hit him non-stop.

The man began to run as the wind with the pain of the knob and with the fear of the horseman. He was both running and falling frequently, and also feeling that on his face.

He was in profuse sweat; whole of his body was wounded.

He was fully satisfied and he was about to sleep. Finally, he felt sick with his stomach and he began to vomit. Whatever he ate got out of his mouth. The snake also got out with what he ate.

The man who saw that the snake got out of his mouth, kneeled down in front of the horseman. He forgot all his problems. And he said to the horseman:

- Oh, nice and clever man. What sacred hour it was when I saw you. May be I was going to die but you gave me a life. I should beg your pardon. Forgive me for the bad words I uttered for you. I didn't utter those words, my ignorance uttered them. Oh nice and clever man! Forgive me! Forgive me for the words I uttered. The horseman said:

- If I told you that the snake went in your stomach, you would scare. If I told you the snake, you would curdle. If you knew the snake inside you, you would be able to neither eat the apple nor run.

For that reason, I could not have told you why I did like this. On the other hand you were about to die. I could not be a mere spectator.

The man who was saved from the snake prayed for him:

- Oh, my dear master! Thank you. May God give you health and happiness! May God give you good luck!

THE MAN WHO CANNOT SEE THE END

There was a man poor and homeless; by all means he was bankrupt. He had no money. Wherever he found a piece of bread, he would take and eat it. He stayed in dark-prisons and was tied with merciless chains. In this prison, he set his eyes on other's meal and their portions. Now, the men in prison regard him as causing trouble for them. He took the portion whoever had.

The men in prison were fed up with the man and they called the guard out.

- Go and tell our greetings to the sultan. We are fed up with that vulgar man. That indiscreet and piggish man had inhabited here. He perches as a fly on all food and moreover without being invited and greeting. What a shameless man he is? The food for sixty people is not enough for him. Whatever you say, he doesn't hear and understand. Everyone will be hungry because of him. Save us from that man.

The understandable guard transmitted the desire of the convicts to the qadi (judge) . He expressed the complaints of the poor. The qadi called him to his presence. He asked his believable men and understood that the convicts were right.

The qadi rebuked him:

- Just get out of the prison. Go and sit in home.

He answered:

- I am homeless. It is what you give. If you take me out of the prison, I will die of poverty. I am a bankrupt.

The qadi said:

- Prove me that you are bankrupt.

The man said:

- All the men in prison are witnesses.

The qadi said to the insolvent:

- They already complain about you. Are their witnesses acceptable? Whomever qadi asked about his situation they answered it.

- Qadi give up this insolvent. This man can do nothing.

Upon this, the qadi ordered his men:

- Inform barkers. Let no one sell nothing to him; let no one give him any dept.

The barkers caught the man very securely. They had him get on a camel, which was passing from there. The woodcutter shouted but the barkers didn't mind him.

The barkers were walking around the city by playing drums.

- Oh, inhabitants! This man is insolvent and he has nothing. Let no one lend him even a stamp. This man is forger. Do not cooperate with him. Don't believe him even if he brings you an ox to sell. If you are cheated and tend to bring a suit against him he won't be put into prison. Look him thoroughly, identity him.

Thus, they walked around from the morning to the evening. When it was evening, they took the insolvent from the camel. The owner of the camel said to the insolvent man:

- My home is too far to hear. It is too late too. Give me at least money for a palm of straw.

The insolvent man turned to the owner of the camel and said:

- Are you stupid? Why did we walk around until that time? Where was your mind? Didn't you hear what the barker said, "this man is insolvent, and he has nothing"? Don't believe him". I think you are too rapacious. Your ear is full of rapaciousness too so that you didn't hear what they said. Go away.

The owner of the camel who heard those words stood petrified with empty hands.

THE CHILDREN ARE INNOCENT

There was a sheik known for his generosity. For that reason he was always indebted. He borrowed ten thousands of liras from the rich and gave it to the poor. Besides, he founded a dervish lodge and sacrificed his life, his prosperity and his dervish lodge for the sake of God.

The indebted sheik behaved like this for years. He was borrowing money from people and giving it to people as if it was his duty. In order to be a great man in his death day, he planted different seeds until his death.

Meanwhile, when the signs of death emerged in his body, the indebted people gathered around him. Sheik was dissolving day by day as a candle. The indebted people gave up hope, they were sour-faced they got more sorrowful.

Sheik said:

- Look at the ones who are suspicious. Does not God have four hundred dinar golden?

Meanwhile a child from outside shouted by saying "halva" with the hope of earning money.

The sheik said to the servant:

- Go and buy the whole halva let the indebted people eat it and not look at me painfully even a short time.

The servant immediately got out in order to buy halva. He asked to the boy how much he would pay for the whole halva. The boy answered:

- Half and some dinar.

- No, don't want so much from Sufis. I give you half dinar now so do not complain.

He got him put the halva to the plate and brought and put the plate in front of the sheik.

The sheik said to the indebted:

- Come on, eat that graced halva.

When the plate became empty, the boy took it and said:

- Oh, clever man! Give me my money.

The sheik sad:

- Where can I find money from? I am an indebted man on the other hand and I am dying.

The boy threw the plate to the floor with his grief he began to scream. He began to cry with that pain "I wish bought my feet were broken, I wish I had gone to boiler room so that I would not be able to come here".

Many people came there upon hearing the scream of the boy. The boy said:

- Oh, bad sheik! My master will certainly kill me. If I go near him with an empty hand, he will kill me. Are you satisfied with that?

The indebted people turned to sheik and said:

- What kind of a game it is. You spent our prosperity; you will die indebted to us. In spite of this fact why did you make injustice to another one?

The boy cried by the afternoon. As for the sheik, he closed his eyes and wasn't looking at him. He didn't mind that situation. He took his head inside of quilt. He was deserted and quiet from the gossips and condemnation of people.

It was afternoon. The servant brought a plate of gold that a generous person gave. A rich person knew the situation of the sheik and sent him a present. There was four hundred dinars in one corner of the plate and in one side, there was a half dinar covered with paper.

The servant came and put that plate in front of the sheik. When the cover was held the miracle of sheik was seen. All of them screamed.

- Oh, leader of the sheikhs and shahs what was that? What a secret is it? Oh master of secret owners! We could not know. Forgive us. We complained in vain.

The sheik said:

- I declared all those words lawful to you the secret was that I desired from God. God showed me the right way. That dinar actually it was a small quantity. But it coming depended on boy's crying. If the boy selling halva didn't cry, sea of grace wouldn't burst.

THE THIEVES AND THE SULTAN

Sultan Mahmut came across with a group of thieves while he was walking around the city alone. One of the thieves asked:

- Oh man! Who are you?

He answered:

- I am one of you.

Even though they never saw him they didn't deal with him with the idea of he was a friend of the others. The idea of 'if he is a foreigner, could he come near a community he had never known and say T am one of you" relaxed all of them. They didn't deal with him agreed and left him aside. One of them said:

- Oh the officious in trick and regularity! Come on let everyone show his own skills; let's know how skilful everyone is. Another one said:

- I have such a skill with my ears that I understand whatever a dog says when it barks.

The others by not taking him serious said:

- It is at most two flats.

Another one said:

- All my skill is with my eye. Whomever I see at night in the dark, without doubt, I can remember him in daylight.

Another one said:

- All my skill is with my arm. I can make a hole on the walls with a power.

Another one said:

- God gave me such a nose that I penetrated the mystery of 'people are like minerals'. How much money is there in the earth, which mineral is kept secretly, will it cost be more than itself. I immediately understand those. I can smell the earth like Mecnun (the lover of Leila) and can choose the earth of Leila without hesitating. I smell every shirt and understand is Joseph of devil inside of it.

Another one said:

- My skill is with my hand. I can throw lasso until the top of the mountain. As Ahmet: he threw a lasso to the sky and it reached to Kaaba. My lasso also reaches to the far away lands.

They eventually said:

- Oh a faithful and great friend, tell me what your skill is.

Sultan Mahmut said:

- All my skill is with my beard so that: when they give the criminals to the executioner, when beard moves they be saved from both punishment and death. They are neither sorrowful nor in grief.

- You are our leader, our safety will be with the help of you in the gratitude day, there is not even a piece of your skill with another one, they said. They pronounced Sultan Mahmut as the leader of themselves.

Later, they set forth and began to walk toward the court in order to rob it. Meanwhile, a dog barked at the right side of them.

The thief who can understand what the dog says:

- The dog says that the sultan is with you. The one throwing the lasso threw it to a high place, and all of them climbed there. The smelling one always smelled all around and said: -Here we found it. There is a unique treasure there by showing the wall of the treasure of sultan. The one making hole made a hole on the wall, they got in, each of them took whatever they could then they left and returned.

Sultan noted the ways they passed, the futures and appearance of the thieves and what each of them took, in his mind, when they fell asleep he sincerely left them and returned to his court. He sent guards, watchmen and a group of soldiers who were brave by showing where the thieves were. They caught the thieves and brought to the presence of sultan. All of them were whimpering moreover, they were astonished. No one had seen them and it hadn't been even a day after theft. They were caught by the soldiers

As soon as the one whomever he sees at night remembers him in day light raised his head and looked at the sultan's face, remembered him. Turning to his friends:

- Oh! Sultan is our skilful friend who was with us at night. Here is the sultan who is said to be everywhere. I will desire his community and present intercession. And he said:

- You are the sun of life in the dooms day. Oh sincerely walking sultan! Time is over. Be kind, and move your beard. All of us showed our skills up, however these skills only raised our unluckiness, tied out legs and we got worse. The words of the one who remembers what he saw at night were useful. Already the skills of others were like the devils that tricks people. Whatever to see the face of sultan is different. And sultan is only ashamed of him. They were forgiven.

SULTAN AND SHAHZADAH

Once, a sultan had a brave son. This young shahzadah (prince; a Sultan's son) both knew using weapon well and was loved very much by everyone with his morals and beauty.

One day, sultan saw in his dream that his son had been death. He was very sorrow. Suddenly everything has lost their meaning for him. Sorrow and grief had covered all his life now. His heart was so full with pains that he had been bored of his life.

But, it was only a dream. He woke up. When he regained his consciousness, he became very happy, so that he had never been so happy in his life. Sultan, who was going to die with his sorrow in his dream, was now gong to die with his happiness.

Upon his dream that he saw, the sultan decided to have his son married for his descend to continue. He thought like this "if my son dies as I saw in my dream his son, that is my grandchild, can substitute for him".

Sultan began to look for a beautiful good- tempered and a moral girl without wasting time. He searched and eventually found a daughter of a man who was poor but known for his honesty.

The people in the court didn't like that news. His wife objected and said:

- There should be equality in a marriage. What kind of equality this is. You make a mistake. You are going to have our son married to a poor one.

Upon this, sultan said:

- It is a sin to look down on a pure and innocent person to call her poor. Her heart is rich. Richness of a heart is a virtue of God to his lovely man.

His wife continued her objection and said:

- What will such a poor person bring as a trousseau? Nothing, but if he marries to rich one, cities, castles, pearls and gold will be ours.

The sultan got angry at that idea of his wife and he rebuked her and said:

- I am decisive. It is best and most auspicious marriage.

At the end of that discussion, the sultan was dominative. He had his son married to that noble and honest girl.

The beauty of the bride was really unique. She had a face, which reflects the beauty of sun's rise. Her moral was also too well to explain. Finally shahzadah and that beautiful and moral girl got married. Now, the happiness of sultan doubled. He was happy and comfort.

There was a magician woman in that country. She also loved the son of the sultan that is shahzadah. Se was jealous of his marriage and enchanted him.

This magician had been effective. Shahzadah fell in love with that ugly and old magician. He gave up his beautiful wife and everything.

He kissed her shoes by the effect of his love to that ninety years old magician. The old woman entirely influenced him.

Shahzadah had been captive to her exact a year. That one year in which shahzadah lived with that old woman he got thinner and became exhausted. But he was unaware of everything by the effect of his love to the magician.

On the other hand, the world had been a place of misery for sultan. He had been helpless. He was praying day and night and sacrificing. He was helping the poor and looking for a cure for his son to be saved from the magician. However, in spite of those, the love of shahzadah to magician woman was rising day by day.

Sultan understood there was a divine secret with that occasion and there was no cure apart from praying and begging. He was always praying by prostrating himself. At the end of sultan's continually prayers, another master magician visited the sultan.

Sultan said to the master magician:

- My son left hone and had been ruined.

The master magician said:

- I have come to save him. There is not any other magician to deal with him among all magicians. There am only me. Only I can be superior to that old magician. Forwhy that information was transmitted to me from far away. I have come to break the magic of that old woman. I have come for him not to go pale. Go to the graveyard at dawn. Open that grave there. You will see a knotted rope in it. Bring it to me.

Sultan did what the master magician said. Magician opened knots. He said shahzadah from the old woman from the old woman. When shahzadah regained his consciousness, he ran towards his father's court without wasting time. He kneeled in front of his father and kissed the flour.

Sultan who was happy for his son to be saved from old magician ordered a public celebration. All people enjoyed themselves during a long time. Wife of shahzadah that is who could not attain her desire and poor, had been happy to.

Magician woman also died of her sorrow. She delivered both her ugly face and bad-temper to Azrael. Shahzadah could never understand how he could fall in love with that old and ugly woman.

THE STORY OF A WATER CARRIER

Once, there was a water carrier who was earning his life by carrying water with his donkey. The donkey of him had been like a circle because of the loads on it back. There were hundred of wounds on it back because of heavy loads. It was as if looking forward it death day.

Let alone the barley, he could not satisfy itself even with dry grass. He was suffering much from the wounds on it back as it was carrying heavy load. On the other hand, it owner was hitting him with an iron needles. A person who took care of the horses of sultan in the court felt pity for it when he saw the donkey. He came near it owner, greeted him and asked how he was. Later he asked:

- Why is that donkey double up?

The owner of the donkey said:

- It is because of my poverty, master. I cannot find even straw for it.

The man said:

- Give it to me for a few days. Let me feed it in the shed of sultan so that it can gain power.

The water carrier gave the donkey to the official of court's shed. The official took him to the court shed. The donkey was astonished when it saw Arabic horses, which were fed with much nutrition, well fed, annealed and beautiful. The floor where the horses stood was cleaned and watered. The straw and barley, which were their food, were being given punctually. It couldn't bear when it saw that they were curried with currycomb and cleaned well, it said by rising it head.

- Oh, my great God! I am a donkey but am not I a creature that you created? Why am I so bewildered, my back is full of wounds. Why am I thin? Why am I looking forward to death every minute for the pains on my back and hunger? The situation of the horses is perfect, so why are grief and bad luck only for me?

Meanwhile, after some time war was declared. Arabic horses were saddled, belts were tied up they were taken to war. In the war, they were wounded with arrows of the enemies. All their bodies were wounded with wounds. When they were back from war they were wounded. The survivor Arabic horses were exhausted and fell to the floor after entering the shed. Their keepers were opening their wounds with sharp knives and taking wounds out of their bodieWhen the donkey saw those, it said:

- Oh, my great God! I am pleasant with my poverty and health. I neither want this good nutrition nor ugly wounds.

EBUBEKIR

Sultan of Harzemshah declared war against Sebzvar city. He won that war upon this, the masters of the city, which was ruined and lost the war, came to the presence of sultan and said:

- Oh, lion-tempered! All we got is yours. Allow it to us for a short time. Have us wear earrings to our ears and make us your slave. But please forgive our life.

Sultan:

- I only desire one thing from you. If you do not bring it, I misbehave you so badly that I cultivate all of you as crops. Neither your taxes nor your begging will be useful then.

The comers looked at each other's faces and began to wait the sultan to pronounce what he wants with excitement.

- You will bring me any Ebubekir as a present. That is all. Or else, there is no safety for you from that situation, said Muhammad Alp Ulu Serzemsah.

They answered:

- Oh our sultan, can there be any sand dry in the river? Let's scatter bags of golden for your sake and do whatever you want. However do not desire Ebubekir from us. How can we find Ebubekir in Sebzvar?

- Oh, Zoroastrians! I am not a child to be deceived by being filled with admiration of gold and silver. As long as you don't bring me a present named Ebubekir, nothing you do will be useful.

The citizens sent barkers to everywhere in the ruins, caves, cavities, prosperous places, wreckages and began to look for Ebubekir. They had left no place without looking for during three days and three nights. Eventually, they could find an Ebubekir. He was a passenger. He was suffering from illness in the secluded place of a wreck. They realised him while he was sleeping and said:

- Wake up quickly! Sultan wants you. Our city will be saved with the help of you.

The man said:

- If I had foot and had the ability to walk I would already not stay here and go wherever I could. Would I stay in that country of enemy? I would run to the city of lovers.

But nobody listened to him. They brought a stretcher, which was used to carry corps, and had he lied on it. He was taken to the presence of Harzemsah by the carriers.

Ebubekir said to sultan that:

- Prophet says that "God doesn't take care your features, he only takes care your hearts. And God says 'I take care of your heart. I even don't care your worships and giving gold'". You assumed your heart as a heart gave up looking for heart-owners. Heart is such a creature that seven hundreds of them are missed in it as those seven skies. Do not call those hurt hearts, as hearts, do not look for Ebubekir in the city. Heart owner is a mirror of six sided. God takes care for that mirror in six sides. As long as that heart owner becomes a means, he doesn't care. He becomes intercession for whom he accepts, denies whom he denies. He doesn't give portion without prophet's existence. He leaves his gift to prophet's hand and gifts to his hand.

- Oh the sultan of the sultans! I brought you a heart there is not a better of it in Sebzvar. Everything is all right for the sake of it.

THE INSANE OF THE CITY

A man wanted to get married. However, his mind was confused about this subject. He wanted to counsel a person who was experienced in those matters. One day, he revealed his problem to his friend.

- I have a difficult problem. I look for a brilliant person. Do you know anyone like this?

His friend said:

- I know. There is a man pretending to be insane in our city. However, he is not mad actually, he is a brilliant. Only he can deal with that occasion.

The man asked:

- So how can I found him?

His friend answered:

- Look there, he is playing among the children and made a horse with bamboo. Don't take it into consideration that he plays games like children. He decides correctly. He is a piece of fire in intelligence. He is a man of genius.

The man who wants to learn the situation of the man went near the man who turns the bamboo into horse who was deeply admired. By calling him out, he said:

- Oh man playing games as children! Ride your horse towards here.

The man came near him by riding his bamboo horse and said:

- Hurry up! Let my horse not kick you. What do you want? My horse is a bit bad- tempered.

- I want to marry to a woman from that city. Which of them is suitable for me?

The man, on the other hand trying to calm his bamboo horse down, said:

- There are three kinds of woman in the world. Two of them are worth, problematic. The third one is an attainable treasure. If you marry to the first one, she becomes yours by all means. If you marry to the second, half a-of her becomes yours and the other half leaves you. As for the third type, keep it in your mind that she never becomes yours. Did you get it? Now my horse became more bad-tempered. I am going.

The man went by riding his bamboo horse. He was now among th children. The problematic youth addressed him again.

- Come and explain your words some more. Which of those three kinds of woman shall I choose?

The man pretending as an insane said:

- A virgin girl who had never got married becomes yours by all means. You can be detained from unhappiness and grief with her. The woman whose half is yours is a widow. The woman who can never be yours is a woman with children.

The youth asked again:

- Oh clever man! I have one more question to ask.

- Ask then, be quick because a child kept my ball in the yard.

The youth:

- I could not understand. How can this madness and such extend of mind be associated with each other? You are as a son how can you behave as an insane?

The inhabitants of that city want me to be qadi. I told them that I would not be qadi. They said me "no, there is no other man as brilliant as you". For that reason, I pretend to be insane. Or else they would have me be qadi unwillingly.

THE DIAMOND

One day, when sultan entered to the council, he saw that all the prominent people of the country came together. He took out a diamond and handed it to the chess. Sultan asked:

- What kind of a diamond is it, what is it value?

The chess took it and looked. He said:

- It is a very valuable diamond.

When sultan said:

- Now break it, the chess said:

- How can I break it? I am a person who wants the welfare of your belonging and treasure. How can I consider worthy of such a priceless diamond to disappear.

Sultan admired the word of chess. He gave him cloth as clothe. And he took the pearl from him. Later, he had the event forgotten by mentioning another subject with the others. He gave the diamond to curtain raiser and said:

- If there is a volunteer to buy it, how much does he pay for it?

Curtain raiser said:

- This diamond is as valuable as the half our country. May God protect our country from all devils!

When sultan ordered him to break it, he said:

- Oh my sultan whose sword shines as sun. It is a pity to break and divide it into pieces. Let alone it value, look at it brightness. Even the radiance of day is in accordance with it. Now can dare to break it? How can I be an enemy of Sultan's treasure?

Sultan presented him cloth and raised his income. He began to praise his intelligence. After a while, he gave the diamond to another man, examined him too. He said the same thing, also the other men in the council. He gave clothes to each of them and gifted. He made those vulgar people out of way and threw them into well. All of fifty or sixty people imitated the chess. Actually, the value of the world is imitation but each imitator is wasted in the examination.

Only Eyaz (Man's name) who was waiting at the corner was left. Sultan said him by giving the diamond to him:

- Oh Eyaz! Tell me what the value of such a bright and beautiful diamond is.

He answered:

- It is more than I can tell my lord.

Sultan said:

- So, break it.

There were stones in Eyaz's pockets. He immediately broke the diamond, divided it into pieces. All of the men screamed.

They said:

- What fearlessness it is. Who breaks that beautiful diamond is unbeliever.

All men in that community didn't keep the order of sultan for their badness.

Eyaz said:

- Oh famous prominent. Is order of sultan or the diamond superior? You don't mind even the order of sultan. I don't take my eyes from sultan. I don't fear as the unbeliever. A person who chooses and leaves aside the order of sultan has no value. Put the rose coloured toy on back and remember who gives colour to them. If you are not way layer, do not believe in colour and perfume as woman.

Upon those words, those prominent men bowed their heads in order to make an excuse for their mistakes to sultan. They sighed hundred times. Sultan gave order to sultan his old executioner.

- Take those men away from my door. Those vulgar men are not worthy to that position. For a stone, they rejected my order. My order became vile for a pointed cup for this kind of troublemakers.

Upon this, merciless Eyaz stood up, ran to the throne of sultan and said him:

- My sultan, even the sky admires the management of the great sultan like you. The generous take their generousness; the happy take their happiness from you. Oh owner of kind and generous. The mistake and insolence of those guilty people result from the wealth of your forgiveness. Oh forgiving person! Forgive them. You are the prominent in gifting. I am guilty. Forgive, forgive, and forgive...

THIEVES AND GARDENER

A gardener saw three thieves entering his garden. One of them was a poor clergyman, the other was sheriff and the third one was a dervish. All of them were disloyal and unjust.

The gardener said himself:

- It is necessary to catch but I cannot deal with all of them by only myself. For that reason, I should separate them. Let me separate them to different parts and fight them when each of them is alone.

Gardener went near three men friendly. He welcomed all of them. Turning to dervish:

- My house is there. Go there and bring my carpet. Let's put it under a tree and sit on it.

Dervish went, now the gardener and two friends were together.

Gardener said to clergyman by turning him:

- You are a clergyman. This friend of yours is Seyyid that is a person from prophet's generation. We do our duties with your fatwa. How can a dervish who earns his life from other people be friend with noble people like you? Now, when he comes, dismiss him. And you can be guest of my garden for a week. What a garden means. Let all be yours.

The gardener made them suspicious and cheated them. When dervish came, they dismissed him. He stood up and went.

The gardener took a big stick to his hand and ran after dervish. When he caught him:

- Oh, dog! What kind of dervish you are! When you find a chance, you steal. Did they tell you those in order to be a dervish? And he began to beat him.

As the gardener caught him alone, he bet him thoroughly. He had him sub-death. And he wounded his head.

Dervish said:

- All happened to me, my friends; you can experience the same too. You regarded me as a foreigner but I am not more foreigner than this gardener to you.

After beating the dervish, gardener came near the others. Addressing Seyyid he said:

- Oh Seyyid! Go to my house, I rolled dough thin for lunch. Tell the servant to give them to you.

The gardener who sent Seyyid said to the clergyman by turning to him:

- Oh clever man! You are brilliant of religious. It is obvious that you have intelligence and point of view.

Your friend says that he comes from prophet generation. However, is it clear that who his ancestors are? Nowadays, lots of people claim that they come from prophet's generation.

The gardener said some more words. The clergyman listened to him. His friend began to dislike Seyyid. The gardener stood up and went his home.

To Seyyid he said:

- Oh donkey! Who invited you to that garden? From whom did you inherit that theft? Lion looks like. Tell me from which point of view do you resemble to prophet.

After those words the gardener bet the thief who claimed himself to be Seyyid. Thief called the clergy man in exhausted mood and said:

- Now you are alone. Be careful.

After the gardener dismissed both of the thieves came near the clergyman. By attacking him with a stick, he said:

- Are you a clergyman there is a big difference. Oh shameless man! Where did you get theft fatwa?

The clergyman was beaten. On the other hand, he was saying:

- You are right beat me. This is what a man who leaves his friend deserves.

FEAR

One day, a man sheltered a home. He was very pale by the effect of fear. His teeth and hands were whimpering. His lips were purple. He ran so much while escaping that he was so exhausted to stand up.

The landowner asked:

- What happened? What is matter with you? Your hands are whimpering. Why did you escape? Why are you so pale?

The man said:

- They catch all donkeys outside today in order to entertain cruel sultan.

The landowner could not understand those words.

- All right that is none of your business. Excuse me but why are you sad and afraid? You are not a donkey.

The man said:

- You are right, but you don't know something. The helpers of sultan are so interested with that duty, that they cannot distinguish human being from donkey. The man, who cannot distinguish, can also take the owner of donkey by regarding him as a donkey.

The landowner couldn't say anything against those words.

BAD VOICED MUEZZIN

Once, there was a bad voiced muezzin in a city. Where he works, Muslims were less in number than the Christians.

Some said to muezzin:

- Do not call the prayer with that bad voice, there can be reactions.

But muezzin was very obstinate. For that reason, he didn't mind any warnings. He went on calling to prayer in this way.

One day, a Christian came to seem with a suit in his hand. And an old friend of him brought a suit and halva for muezzin.

- Where is muezzin? His azan and voice comfort people.

The people said astonishingly:

- Are you kidding? Be careful. How can his voice comfort people?

- His voice came until church. I have a beautiful daughter. She has desired to be Muslim for a long time. Whatever we did, who could not change her mind. She didn't give up the idea of being Muslim. While I was thinking what to do, the voice of muezzin was heard from church. My daughter asked what that bad voice was. And she added. "I have never heard such a bad voice like that in my life".

Her daughter said her:

- It is azan voice. It is a Muslim custom; they call Muslims to pray with that voice.

My daughter could not believe. Her faith for Islam was destroyed. She became sad. She lost her desire for Islam.

She gave her mind up being Muslim, and I was relaxed I want to find him and give those presents.

FREEDOM, FREEDOM, FREEDOM

Here was green place from inside of which water was flowing with a gentle. A mouse, which lives in the mossy stones in the river shore, would wake up with this water gurgling.

It was same in that morning too. He opened his eyes. He got out of stones. There was an alone frog in the river shore. It said:

- Good morning, frog brother. What a nice day, isn't it? Fortunately, I saw you. Or else I would be too bored of loneliness.

The frog was also suffering from loneliness. It said to the mouse:

- I didn't know that you lived here. I thought there was nobody here. But you were here. So, we are neighbours.

After that day, the mouse and the frog established a very good friendship. Their friendship was gradually improving day by day. It was such extend that, when it was evening, one of them would go into the stones and the other into the deep of water, but could wait impatiently until morning.

This could not go on like that. Forwhy they missed each other too much during night.

They should have found a solution to that situation.

The mouse found the solution. He said to the frog:

- My dear friend. We separate in nights. We miss each other. We had better find a rope. Let's tie one side of it to your foot and the other side to my tail. When it is night, as soon as we miss each other we can pull the rope. Thus, we can always meet.

The frog accepted that offer. Two of them were tied with one rope.

A few days passed. A crow saw the mouse; he burrowed between stones by setting trap.

When it was evening, the mouse turned his home. The crow didn't miss this opportunity. It flew as soon as he caught the mouse. Of course, the frog was going with them. There was nothing to do.

IS SHOUTING USEFUL?

The caravan took way all day long. When It was night, it stayed in a cool place. Everyone fell asleep with fatigue.

The guard of caravan was also among the sleeping people. A thief utilised that opportunity and robbed the caravan. He buried the goods he stole. When it became day, people of caravan make up only to see that their goods and silvers were all stolen.

The people were discussing the situation by coming together. They called the guard of the caravan. They said:

- Oh guard of caravan! What happened to our belongings? Where didn't they go?

The guard said in order to hinder that he slept he said:

- In an unexpected time, thieves whose faces were covered came and took everything in front of me.

People of caravan asked:

- Oh cowered guard! What were you doing while they were stealing our goods? Why are you here? Aren't you a guard?

The guard said:

- I was alone. I couldn't deal with them. What could I do against lots of armed men?

- So why didn't you wake us up?

The guard said by stemming?

- Just at the moment I was going to shout, they threat me. They said, "if you do not shout up we will kill you". Then, I couldn't shout if you want let me now shout.

THE PRAY FOR THE BAD

Once, there was a preacher. When he sat to the desk he used to pray for the bad, not for the good. He prayed like "Oh my God, please mercy to all the bad, the intriguer, the brigand, the unbeliever the all bad churches and synagogues."

No one from the community had ever come across with such a thing. Why was that preacher praying like that because they were very curious about that subject?

One day they said: "oh the preacher why do you always pray for the bad not for the good? We came across such a thing for the first time".

The preacher said: "once I suffered so troubles and pains, I suffered a lot I was beaten by them they behaved me so badly and tyrannised me so badly that they diverted me to be a good person. They saved me from being a bad person. That is, they are the ones who caused my safety. For that reason I regard to pray for them as a duty. If it hadn't been them, perhaps I wouldn't be honest.

What would you do if you were in my shoes? What would you do instead of praying for them?"

THE ILL TEACHER

That day, the students didn't want to study. But how would they provide that? The most brilliant of that decided and said:

- Let's say our teacher: "today, you are so pale. This situation results from cold or malaria. If he is seized in pane, he goes mad. If the second, third and forth friend of us goes one like that, the teacher will think that he is really ill.

All the children said:

- Well done! What an excellent idea.

- Later, they came to an agreement among them. One would reveal their secret to another one.

When it was morning, they went to school from their homes with that idea. All of them began to wait the most excellent child. He came. Greeted the teacher and said:

- What is the matter with you teacher? You seem pale.

The teacher said:

- No, I am not ill. I don't have ache. Sit down. Do not speak nonsense.

He spoke like that but he secretly began to be suspicious. Another child came. When he said the same, his suspicious began to rise. The teacher was also surprised by his condition. He thought himself ill with the fear; he set forth to his home after he wore his cloth tightly. He was walking on the other hand he was saying:

- Oh my God! Why didn't my wife realise my illness. She sent me to job when I was ill. I think that woman doesn't love me. She wants to get rid of me.

He went home with those thoughts, opened the door harshly. The children were also after him. His wife said:

- What is the matter, Why did you come early? Is there something bad?

The teacher s-Are you blind? I am ill. Look at my face it is so pale.

His wife said:

- Oh teacher, you have no problem. You worry for no reason unnecessarily.

The teacher got angry.

- Disloyal woman! You are lying. Cannot you see my position? I am trembling. If you are blind, what is my guilty?

His wife said:

- Oh my God! Did you go mad? Let me bring a mirror so that you can see yourself.

- Get out! You already get rid of me. Prepare my bed so that I can rest.

The woman helplessly brought the bed. She was saying secretly:

- It is no use. He doesn't listen to me. He is living with an apprehension. If I say "you are not ill", he will find me guilty.

She prepared her husband's bed. The teacher was laid up. He began to complain.

The children were regretful and they said:

- We have done all of these. We are guilty enough to be put into prison.

As the teacher was ill, the school was holiday.

Children went home and started to play games.

Their mothers said:

- Although it is weekday, why do you play game?

The children answered: -Our teacher has been ill and he is in bed. We are not guilty. Their mother said:

- I think you are lying. Tomorrow we will go to the school and ask.

In the morning the other of the children came to the teacher's home. The teacher slept as a seriously ill person. He was sweaty with the weight the guilt. He took the guilt until his head. He was slowly complaining. The entire women were surprised.

- What is the matter teacher? What is your illness?

The answer of the teacher was astonishing.

- I swear I wasn't aware of it either. Those children informed me my illness.

THE STORY OF A POET

A poet brought a poem to sultan with the hope at going sultan's favour, go gain office. Sultan was generous. He ordered the man to be given a thousand of golden and other offers.

His chess said:

- It is not enough. Give him ten thousand golden so that he can be happy. It is not much but few for such a generous sultan to give such an important poet.

Sultan gave the poet ten thousand golden and clothes appropriate for him. Poet was thankful and he said:

- With whose efforts did those much process happened? Who praised me to sultan?

They said him:

- It happened with the suggestion of a chess named Hasan whose name and temper are pure and beautiful.

Upon this, the poet wrote a long ode that is a praise poem, for chess whose name and temper are beautiful. He took it to the home of chess. After a few years, the poet again became poor because he suffered in poverty. He said to himself:

- It is useful to try generous person who helped me in my scarcity times. I should again take my need to the previously tried door.

The poet came once more to generous sultan in order to get gift. In the poem that he took to sultan, he was thanking to sultan who gifted greatly and he was pointing out that gift and help had not died yet. He presented it to sultan with hope of getting the tip and gift he got a few years ago. This poem was full of very beautifully written lines as pearls with hope and tip.

The habit of sultan was to give poets a thousand gold.

He said:

- Let this poet be given a thousand of gold.

But unfortunately, this time old chess was not there. A miserly chess was promoted to the place of old chess. He said:

- My sultan, we have too much expanses. We cannot give a thousand of golden to that poet for only one poem. Fifty-five golden is enough.

The people there said:

- This generous sultan gave a thousand golden to that poet in time of old chess.

Sultan said to his chess.

- All right, do whatever you want. But, in any case, satisfy him, because he illustrates us beautifully.

After that, chess began to get the poet to wait. Meanwhile, seasons changed. The poet became older while waiting for a gift. The attitude of the chess frustrated him.

The poet said:

- If you want to give golden, at least curse me so that my life can get free of you. Let me stand up and go.

After that the chess gave him twenty-five gold. The poet was surprised and he was absorbed in thoughts. The first gold was given without having been waited. It was too much. The gold given now was both late and little. That generous and clever chess and misery chess came for the place of him.

The poet turned to the ones in the palace and said:

- Oh, friends! Where that bad-tempered chess did came from. What is the name of that robber?

The people there said:

- It is Hasan.

The poet expressed his emotions like that:

- Oh my God! The name of the older one was Hasan too. How can such a thing be? If sultan listens to that man's words he disgraces both himself and his country.

WHO IS OLDER?

A camel, an ox and a ram found a bouquet of gross.

The ram said:

- If we share it among us, it will satisfy none of us. Let our oldest eat it because it is better. Forwhy it is an old custom to respect elders.

The dams later said to the ox and camel:

- Friends! Now that, we found such a food, let all of us say our beginning of life. Let's see which of us is older, and when it is understood, let's not speak any more. Let me say first, my beginning to eat grass is hosted on the time of dam that is sacrificed for the sake of prophet Isa.

The ox said:

- When, I was young, I was the partner of the ox, which Adam ploughed. Remember that the ancestor of human beings. Adam was ploughing the earth and planting crop I was broken in the same bullock.

The camel was shocked after hearing those words from dam and ox. It inclined it head took the bouquet of grass from the floor. Raised it up and ate without saying anything.

- It is not necessary for me to give an exact date. When I have such an enormous body and such along body, everyone knows that I am not smaller than you. Every clever man knows that my creature is older than yours.

SUCHLIKE LOVE

Once, there was a lover. He loved his beautiful darling for years, waited in order to meet her and become the slave of sultan of sultans.

A seeking person finds finally. Forwhy the comfort is resulting from patience. One day his lover said him:

- Come tonight. I prepared dessert for you. I cooked meals. Wait in the home until midnight. Sit and wait. Before you call me, I will come in the midnight.

The lover man killed as a sacrifice after that good news. He distributed bread to the poor. At night, he went that home which they planned; he thought his darling would keep her promise he began to wait, helplessly. After midnight, his darling kept her promise. But she found her lover sleeping. She cut a piece of his cloth.

- You are not a real lover, you are still a child. Take those walnuts and play with them.

When the lover woke up at dawn he jumped and stood up. He saw that a piece of cloth was cut and walnuts were put into his pocket. He got the message.

Our sultan and love consist of honesty and loyalty from the beginning to the end. Whatever happens to us result from us and ourselves, and he began to cry.

THE ILL MAN

An ill man went to doctor and he said:

- Oh doctor, please take my pulse. Forwhy you can understand the situation of heart with the help of pulse. Because heart is inside, it is not seen the situation of it can be understood by pulse.

Doctor took his pulse. When he understood that there was no hope for him to recover, he said:

- Do whatever you want let your illness in your body be cured. But know that patience and dieting do not cure your illness. Do whatever you want.

The ill man began to walk around the river shore in order to maintain cure for his illness. A dervish was sitting and washing his hands and face.

The ill man saw the nape of dervish he wanted to hit him on his nose. He raised his hand in order to hit him. Because the doctor said him " if you don't do what you like, it becomes a worry for you."

He secretly said" come on and hit him. This patience, this dieting is dangerous. Do not hesitate as the others. Hit thoroughly to him.

When he hit dervish on his nose, a "smack" was heard.

Dervish said:

- Oh immoral man! What are you doing?

Dervish wanted to sock two or three fists, tear out his beard and moustache and he thought "it is not good for me to get into trouble for me as a response to a slap".

When dervish regarded his enemy weak, he changed his mind and said:" Actually I had better sock him a fist". But later "if I sock him the man melts as tin and if sultan commands retaliation, they kill me".

When dervish could not challenge to hit the man, he decided to complain him to qadi. Dervish went near the man. Taking him near qadi by grasping him from his arm and said:

- Have this man to get on a horse and disgrace to the people.

Qadi said:

- My son, first of all, explain the situation thoroughly, what is the matter? Tell thoroughly. Let me decide according to it. Where is the person who hit, he is in an exhausted position, he is like a ghost. Rules are for living people, can they be employed to the death.

Dervish said:

- All right qadi. Do you find it right for this man to hit me when I am innocent?

Qadi said to the guilty man:

- Do you have any money?

The man answered:

- I have five coins.

Qadi commanded:

- Spend three coins of it for you. Give the rest to that dervish.

Meanwhile, the old man had his eyes on the nose of qadi. His nape was better than dervish's nape.

The old man thought, "The blow I gave him is too cheap". He raised his hand, went near qadi. He bowed as if he would whisper something to his ear. Meanwhile slapped him on his nape and said:

- You both share five coins now good bye.

THE STORY OF TRAVELLING

A Jew, a Muslim and a Christian went on travelling together. These three friends reached their destination. A rich person brought them halva as a present.

The Jew and the Christian was suffering of stomach-ache because of their gluttonousness. The Muslim was fast. When it was evening and when halva came the Muslim was very hungry.

The other gluttonous people said:

- We are fully satisfied. Let's put this halva aside, and eat it tomorrow. Let's be patient this night and not eat it.

The Muslim said:

- Let's eat it that night, not put it aside for tomorrow. It is not time to be patient.

The others said:

- You want to eat the halva yourself.

The Muslim made proposal.

- Look friends! Now that we cannot agree, let's share the halva. Whoever wants his portion, let him eat, if he doesn't, let him leave it aside.

And Christian said:

- Give up sharing.

The aim of the Jew and Christian was to leave Turk hungry that night.

Muslim was defeated by them. For that reason, he agreed. By inclining his neck, he said:

- All right, friends.

That night, they went bed and slept. They got up in the morning. They washed their hands and faces. Later, three of them gathered.

One of them:

- Let everyone tell his dream. Whoever has the best dream, let him eat the halva?

They said “all right”. First, Jew began to tell his dream:

- In my dream, I was walking on a way. On the way, I came across with Moses. I fallowed him. We went till Tur Mountain. I was invisible by brilliance. Both Moses and Tur Mountain were invisible. Meanwhile, that blessed shining door was opened. Brilliance got out of brilliance. That second brilliance rose up. It enlightened the sky.

I was lost in the light of second brilliance, Moses was lost too and also Tur Mountain was lost. Briefly, I was in brilliance all night.

Christian began to talk after Jew.

- I saw the prophet Jesus in my dream. I went up to the forth floor of the sky, where the sun is. I witnessed so surprising peculiarities of value of heaven that it is not right to compare what I saw with worldly affairs. Everyone knows that the very high sky is a hundred times larger than that very low world.

After that, it was Muslim’s turn.

- In my dream, my master Muhammad came near me. He said me that Jew talked with Moses who had the honour of talking with God. Christian went up to the forth floor of the sky. Stand up and eat the halva as a person who remained behind and was damaged.

Jew and Christian who heard those words asked:

- So, did you eat the halva?

Muslim said:

- How can I dare not to carry out the order of that blessed man if he tells me to eat the halva. You are Jewish; can you break the order of Moses? You are a Christian; don't you do what Jesus says? I obeyed the order and ate the halva.

Upon this, they said:

- I swear, the dream you saw is a real dream. This dream is a hundred times better than ours.

THE STORY OF REPENTANCE

Once, there was a man named Nasuh. He used to earn his life as a bath attended in woman clothes, in women's bathhouse. Because his face looked like woman face and his voice was like woman voice. He worked as a bath attended for years; no one was suspicious of him. No one could understand his secret.

He used to cover his head by dressing with veil; he used to wear a veil. In this way, he could rub even the daughters of sultans. Sometimes, he used regret, he used to repent, wanted to give up bad attendance but his sinful soul and his patient to woman pretended him.

As Nasuh knew the badness o f that situation, he one day went near a wise person and said:

- Remember me while praying to God.

That wise person learned his secret but didn't reveal it. But he loved eccentrically. He said:

- Oh bad natured person! Let God give you the chance of repentance.

One day, while Nasuh was filling his cup with water in bath, a valuable diamond of sultan's daughter was lost. They closed the door of bad and began to look for it among everyone's belongings. Everyone's possessions were searched but the diamond could not be found. Upon this, they decided to search everyone one by one. They shouted:

- Young or old let everyone take their clothes off.

The servant girls of sultan began to search everyone. Nasuh went a remote place, with his fear. His face was pale and his lips were purple with his fear. He was thinking about his death and was trembling as a leaf.

- My God, I repented many times, promised but late broke them. Eventually, bad luck caught me. If it is my turn to be searched, poor me, what I will do? Let even my enemy not have such a problem and trouble. Pity me my God. It would be better if my mother hadn't given me birth or a lion had eaten me by dividing into pieces.

- Please my God, my time has been shorter. Show generosity. Now, conceal my sin. Now, I repent to all evils. Accept my repentance so that I can make an effort not to break my repentance. If I make a mistake any more, do not accept my repentance.

Nasuh was weeping, seeing Azrael in front of his eyes. He said "oh my God" so many times that the wall began to say "oh my God". While Nasuh was praying a voice was heard:

- Oh Nasuh! We search everyone, now come here.

When Nasuh heard that voice he fainted. He fell down as a cracked wall.

When he was unconscious, his secret reached God. Just at that moment:

- Here is the lost diamonds, some one said.

"Diamond was found" sound was rising up among happy screams, shouts and noises.

Unconscious Nasuh regained his conscious. His eyes were enlightened. He saw good and bright days. Everyone was excusing as they all thought bad things about him. Because as he was very close to sultan's daughter, everyone said "he did it".

Nasuh was the best bath attended of sultan's daughter. He knew every secret of her. Everyone thought "there is nobody closer to sultan than him".

Nasuh said them:

- It is a grace of God to me. Or else, I am a rather worse person than you think. Why do you excuse, because I am the most sinful of all people. Later, someone came and said Nasuh:

- Daughter of sultan calls you. She wants you to wash her.

Nasuh said:

- Get away. Now Nasuh is ill. Run and look another one. I swear I cannot serve her any more. He said to him "I am too sinful, how can I forget that fear and pain? I really repented so I can not break it any more".

THE FOX AND THE DONKEY

Once, there was a donkey. Its back was wounded and it was hungry and thin. It used to walk around the infertile rocky hungry, dirty and homeless until days and nights. There was nothing but water to drink. The donkey was in that sorrowful and mourning country.

There was also a lion there whose all duty was to hunt. It fought with a male elephant; it was wounded and tired and also could not effort to hunt. For a while, it could not go for hunting owing to his fatigue. It was out of food. The animals, which were fed with the lion's remains, were also out of food.

The lion called a fox and said:

- Go, if you see a donkey on the meadow, utter nice words, deceive it and bring it to me. If I eat the donkey and gain power, I can found another hunt. I eat a few of it, so you can eat the rest.

The fox said to the lion:

- At your disposal. Let me bring the donkey here by deceiving it with tricks and cunning. Already to be cunning is my art.

The fox began to run from hill to the river after setting forth. It went near the donkey by greeting it friendly. It became closer to that poor. And it asked:

- How are you in that fertile plain, in that rocky?

The donkey said:

- It does not matter whether I am in grief or in a place as heaven. God gave me my portion. I am thankful to him either in good times or bad times. Forwhy there is worse than worse.

The fox said:

- But it is necessary to look for honest portion. Nothing can be obtained unreasonably. In that condition, it is absolutely necessary to want and look for.

The donkey said:

- A mouthful of bread is not few for a person who wants glory and kingdom. Generous God gives portion to everyone, your nit baring difficulty of working results from your impatience.

The fox said:

- The resignation you talk about is scarce. Only a few people can obtain that resignation. Let them alone and try to earn something even little.

The donkey said:

- I know no better way than resignation to God. We thank him and he gives us more portions.

This speech became longer and longer. Both of them were exhausted of period of question and answer. After that, the fox said to the donkey:

- Do not risk you by your own. The world of God is large. Do not waste your life in that rocky place. There is a very nice meadow in the further, fed you there on the river shore with green gross.

The fox insisted on trick and took the donkey. He took the donkey to the forest for the lion to attack and wound him. The donkey was far from the lion, but the lion could not be patient for the donkey to be closer. Suddenly, it roared strangely but it was not powerful enough to move.

The donkey saw that and escaped until the deep of the mountain.

The fox said to the fox:

- Oh my lord, why could not you patient in the time of fight? If that stupid donkey became closer to you, you could defeat it with a small attack. It was far away, it understood that you would attack and it escaped. Your weakness became obvious.

The lion said:

- I thought my self-powerful and not exhausted. My hunger became unbearable. Now, I became impatient. If you can do, deceive it again and bring here.

The lion said:

- I will do it again, however if I deceive and bring it here, do not waste my efforts by hurrying up.

Upon this the lion said:

- Yes, I am very ill and exhausted. Unless the donkey becomes very close to me I will not move and I will pretend to be sleeping.

The fox set forth again. It went neSr the donkey.

The donkey said:

- It is necessary to refrain from a friend like you. What did I do you that you took me near that dragon?

The fox said:

- What you saw was a dream; it was lion's vision. Or else, I am thin and weak. See I look for my portion there. I would already say you "do not fear if you see such a vision".

The donkey said:

- Oh fox! Get away; let me not see your face. God who made you unlucky also created your face very badly. How can you dare to come near me? You plot against my life obviously by saying "let me take you to the meadow". Whether I am a donkey or the worst and most defective of donkeys, I have a life too. How can I waste my life? I swear, from now on, I will not believe anybody.

The fox said:

- There is no sediment in our innocent hearts. Oh well-meaning donkey! All those result from your groundless fear, or else there is neither a trick nor badness in my heart against you. Do not blame me by being deceived by your own ugly vision. Why do you suppose your lovers bad?The donkey wanted to be away from the fox in order to get rid of it. But it was very hungry. Hunger didn't leave him. Ambition became superior and it patience became weaker. He thought, "even that is a trick, I am about to die of hunger. At least, I can get rid of that hunger. If that life is life, to death is better".

The fox took the donkey near the lion. That brave lion divided the donkey into pieces. The lion went to the river in order to drink water after he satisfied his stomach. The fox made use of that opportunity and ate lungs and brain of the donkey. When the lion came from the river and wanted to continue eating the donkey, it looked for it lungs and brain. But there was neither heart nor lung.

It asked to the fox:

- Where is it lung, what happened to it brain?

The fox answered:

- If it had a brain, would it come near you? What would a clever person who experienced that disturbance, fear and escape do here again?

THE SULTAN AND HIS SLAVE

The sultan had a slave. He was not clever. But he was very ambitious. That slave leaves aside some serve s of the sultan, which sultan considered as trivial and was in deep thought of bad suppositions, bad ideas but thought that bad suppositions and ideas were correct.

The sultan realised that bad habit of the slave. He ordered to his servants:

- Cut down his salary, if he rejects, tell him to erase his name from the list of slaves.

The slave became furious and more severe when he understood that his salary was lower. He decided to write a letter full of hatred to the good sultan.

Before the slave began to write the letter, he went near the chief and said:

- Oh the cook of generous sultan! I see the money, which was cut down from my salary far away from generosity of our sultan.

The cook said:

- I swear, that order cannot be Sultans.

The cook showed him proof but he accepted none of them.

The slave accused the cook by saying "you do that deliberately.

The cook said:

- No we are subordinates.

The slave went a silent place angrily and wrote a letter with anger to the sultan. In that letter, he praised the sultan and mentioned about his generosity. In his letter he said "oh my generous sultan whose palm is more generous than the sea and cloud in meeting the demands of needy people! Cloud gives but it gives in a crying way. But your palm lays the table of food by laughing.

The letter was praising but there was anger also.

They took the letter of the slave to the sultan. The sultan read the letter but did not answer. Silence was the best answer to that stupid.

He was full of ambition and said:

- Why didn't the sultan answer? Or did not they take the letter to him? Perhaps, they deceived me.

The slave who was aware of nothing because of his ignorance accused sometimes the sultan, sometimes the cook and sometimes the person who took the letter. The slave who was in bad ideas wrote a new letter. That letter was full of condemnations, wailing and complaints

That beautiful-faced sultan read that letter but he didn't answer it again, he didn't mind his complaints.

Thus, the slave wrote five letters one after another. Eventually, the court chamberlain said to the sultan:

- My sultan, do not overlook what he said. He is your slave too. it would be good if you wrote an answer. What can you lose if you were kind?

The sultan said:

- It is easy to write a letter but the slave is stupid. And a stupid man is ugly. An ill person makes a hundred people ill, moreover, if he has an illness of stupidity. It is better not to answer such a person.

A PROUD FLY

Once, a fly was wondered proudly and regarded itself as the king of the winged animals. One day, he found himself in a travelling ship. It was shocked and astonished. He sad to himself "oh my God! In an enormous sea, a small man directs an enormous ship, is it possible?"

When the ship approached to the shore, it flew to the earth and perched on a straw on which a donkey previously put it feet and urinated. As the straw was shaking, he realised that what he was shocked in the ship a few minutes ago was happening to him. "Why was I so shocked? Here is the sea and I am a captain of the ship". He became very proud of himself.

WHO IS THE SULTAN?

One day, the sultan comes across with a scholar and asks him whether he wants anything or not. The scholar said: "my sultan we don't except anything from the sultan of world. I have too slaves. Even when they overcome you, how can you look down on me"?

The sultan got very angry upon those words and asked to the scholar: "are you aware of what you are saying? Who are those slaves?"

The scholar said by laughing "one of them is anger, the other one is lust my sultan. There is almost nobody who can not overcome those". As sultan believed him, he realised his mistake and excused to the scholar.

THE PATIENT DONKEY

A dervish set forth a journey. Finally, he became guest in a khan. He had a donkey. He tied the donkey to a shed. He stood the seat of honour table with his friends. He was absorbed in conversation. He remembered his donkey during meal; he turned to the servant of the khan and said:

- Go to the shed. Give it straw and barley.

The servant said:

- It is not necessary for you to tell. It is my job for a long time.

Dervish continued giving advice:

- First, water the barley; because the donkey is old, his teeth cannot cut.

The servant said mourning:

- You speak unnecessarily, I know those works best.

Dervish said:

- Look, first of all take it palan (a broad soft saddle without frame) . Put drug to his wounded back in order to lessen it pain.

The servant said:

- All right, I understood, do not teach me my job. I entertained so many guests like you. All of them were pleasant. I am fed up. Do not speak much; do not give advice to me.

Later, the servant thought to bring barley and straw first of all.

The servant went but he didn't even remember the shed. After he went near his friends he made fun of dervish's speech and entertained himself.

The dervish was very tired and exhausted after a long travel. He was seeing dreams with open eyes. In his dream, his donkey fell into the clutches of a wolf. The wolf was dividing it into pieces from it back and leg.

When dervish woke up and said:

- What nonsense dreams it was, where is that kind servant?

Later, he was seeing dream, he saw that his donkey fell sometimes in a well sometimes in a cavity. He saw various nightmares, jumping out of his bed and praying to God:

- Oh my God! What is the solution to that problem? Does that servant think of misbehaving us?

When dervish was thinking like that, his donkey was in such a situation that I wouldn't wish on my worst enemy. The poor donkey was all night in stones, it palan was contrary, it crupper was broken. It was very tired because of the travel and it was hungry all night.

The poor donkey said and prayed all night:

- Oh my God! Let alone the barley; give me at least a little straw.

The poor donkey hungrily could not sleep by the morning. When it was evening, the servant came he looked for palan and found it. He put it to donkey's back. He hurt the donkey with a sharp stick two or three times as donkey sellers do. The donkey forgot it hunger and was suffering with the dig pain. It jumped and stood up. The poor donkey could not tell it suffering as it could not speak.

The dervish woke up in the morning. He rode his horse and again set forth. The donkey was stumbling in every step. The people who saw the donkey's situation told that it was ill. One of them was looking at his ear and nose, another one was looking at it palate whether there was a wound or not. Another one was looking for a piece of stone in its shoe. The people passing from there asked to the dervish:

- Master, what is the situation of that donkey?

The dervish understood what had happened. That unfair servant left the donkey out of food. When he realised that, he said to the people who asked the situation of donkey:

- If the food of donkey is "la havle" at night, it prostrates like that in daytime.

THE INSOLENT POOR

Once, there was a poor man. He saw Amid, who is the special servant of the sultan, Amid was clad in silk clothes and going on a horse.

The poor raised his head to the sky and asked:

- My God, why don't you learn to help people from that virtuous man? Learn how to have wear and fed from our master.

He was poor, needy, and indigent and had nothing to eat. In winter, he was trembling like a leaf by the cold. That poor who was unaware of himself dared and said something against God helplessly. In deed, he trusted God's endless kindness.

Eventually, one day the sultan accused his closest servant of something. He tied his hand and foot, captured him. The sultan tortured slaves of the sultan by saying "tell me, where the treasure of you master is". If you do not tell where the treasure is I will have your neck and tongue cut.

He tortured them during just a month. The men of the sultan questioned the slaves for long time. Later, they divided them into pieces but none of them revealed the secret of their master. When the poor were sleeping, a voice said him:

- Come, and learn how to be man from the slaves of Amid.

WHO FOUGHT THE THIEF?

One man entered someone's garden and was shaking the tree; he was making the fruit fall down.

The owner of the garden suddenly came and asked:

- What are you doing? Are not you ashamed of God?

The thief said:

- Why do you condemn a person who eats fruit which God created from God's garden? Why do you hurt me? Why don't you want to give the portion God created for his people? Why are you so mean?

Upon those words, the owner of the garden called out his servant.

- Bring me a rope so that I can answer that stupid.

Later, the owner of the garden tied the man to the tree tightly and began to hit him on his back and legs with a big stick.

The thief said:

- Fear from God! You kill an innocent person by fighting and making him shout.

The answer of the garden's owner was ready.

- This stick is the stick of God who I fight is whom God created. And, I am also his person.

Who can condemn a man of God who fights God's creature with God's stick, to an extend God permits?

The thief gave up upon that answer.

- Oh clever man! Okay, I regretted and repented. Leave me now. I really made a mistake.

HOW TO BE SECURED FROM THE RACE OF GOD?

A naive and honest person asked the prophet Jesus "what is the most difficult and harshest thing in the world?" when he came across with him.

The prophet Jesus said him: "oh clever and alert man! The most difficult and the harshest thing in the world is the rage of God".

Upon this, the man said: "you are right. But how can we be secured from the race of God?".

The prophet Jesus answered:

- When you get angry, you can be secured from that race by not being overcome to your desire. The rage and fury of animals is nothing compared to the people. And these kinds of people are the sources of rage and fury. You will escape from them like escaping from a lion and you will never get angry. Already, anger is the Satan.

A STORY OF A NAIVE MAN

An old man went to the palace of prophet Suleiman fussily in the morning.

His face was pale and his lips turned purple because of his sorrow.

Prophet Suleiman said:

- What happened, do you have any problem? You are too flurried.

The man said:

- My master, today I saw Azrael. Azrael looked at me so angrily and so bad that I could not know what to do. I sheltered you.

Prophet Suleiman said:

- So what do you want from me, say it.

The man said:

- My master! Command the wind to take me to India. If that man of you goes there, he can save my life, mercy me.

Prophet Suleiman said:

- All right. He commanded the wind and the wind took that man to India immediately.

Next day, court was held in the presence of Prophet Suleiman. Everyone came to the invitation of Prophet Suleiman. In the course of conversation, Prophet Suleiman asked to Azrael:

- Why did you look sourly at that Muslim? Do you want to deprive him of his property?

Azrael answered:

- Actually, I didn't look at him angrily, I looked at him confusedly. God commanded me to kill him today in India. I thought that even if he had a hundred wigs, he could not reach India, how would I kill him.

THE PROMiSE OF THE DOG

The dog, which was fatigue and in a bad condition in the winter said to itself:

- If I can reach the summer healthy I will establish a shed for myself by trying my best, it is enough, the dog promised to himself. However, when it was summer and the weather tuned out to be well the dog forgot what happened to him in the winter, he didn't even remember. Even if he remembered, he found an excuse "let it alone I have so much time" and persuaded itself. He went on lying lazily "is it time to work rather than lying in the shadow comfortably".

Thus, the winter came again and our dog again began to wait for summer "when it is summer this time I will surely establish that shed".

Of course, when this winter was too cold the dog had no other choice to be frozen.

IMMORTALITY TREE

A scholar told an event similar to a tale during a conversation. According to what he told, there was a tree in India. If a man ate the fruit of that tree, he neither gets older nor dies.

A sultan heard that, he fell in love with that tree and it fruit. He sent one of his men who were clever and reliable to India in order to bring fruit of that tree. The man walked around every part of India in order to find that tree. He went every city to find the fruit.

Whoever he asked, they laughed at him maliciously. They said:

- For the sake of God! Does a clever man look for such a thing? He must be mad.

Some of them beat some of them considered him as mad.

He continually looked for it for years. The sultan sent him goods and money for him to find what he was looking for. But he could get no result of what he looked for. He decided to turn back. He was both crying and walking. On the way to return, there was sheik whose name and fame he had heard. The man said helplessly:

- Let me go to presence of him, perhaps, he can help me.

He went to the presence of sheik tearful. He burst into tears. He said:

- My master. Mercy and help me. I am too helpless.

Sheik said:

- Tell me your problem. What do you want?

The man said:

- My master, the sultan gave me a work to find a tree. There is a unique tree. Is fruit gives immortality? I looked for it for years but I could find nothing instead of mocking glance of others and insult. That is my problem.

Sheik laughed and said:

- Are you looking for that tree now?

- Yes, master.

- Oh naive man! What you look for is the knowledge tree. It is knowledge of a scholar. Go and tell our sultan to stand as a protector of knowledge and scholar.

The man left sheik happily and set forth immediately.

THE LANGUAGE OF BIRDS

One day, a man went near prophet Moses and said:

- Oh Moses! Teach me the language of animals. Let me hear the words of animals so that I can draw a lesson from them. Perhaps, animals have abilities, which we don't know.

Prophet Moses said to the man:

- Give up that desire, because to understand their language has some dangers. Want drawing lesson and ability from God.

Although prophet Moses warned the man against that situation, the man focused on it more. Already, human being focuses on what he has been forbidden more.

The man said:

- Oh Musa! Do not deprive me of my desire. It doesn't befit your kindness. I become so sad.

Prophet Musa said:

- Oh my God! I think Satan deceives that naive man. If I give what he wants, it will be bad for him, if I don't, I will hurt him.

When he was directed to "teach", Musa called the man. He said:

- Look! What you want will harm you. Give up that desire. Be afraid of God. Satan has deceived you.

The man said:

- At least teach me the language of the rooster and the dog, which lies in front the door and guards home.

Prophet Moses said:

- Alright, it is your choice. Now go. From now on you will learn their language.

The man waited in front of the door with the anxiety whether he could really learn their language or not.

When the servant was shaking the tablecloth, a big piece of bread fell to the floor. The rooster immediately took the piece of bread. The dog rebuked the rooster:

- You made a mistake. Forwhy you can eat small pieces also, but I can not. You ate the bread, which was my portion.

The rooster said to the dog:

- Stop talking. The horse of the landowner will die tomorrow. You can eat bones satisfactorily. Don't be sad.

When the landowner heard those words, he immediately sold the horse. As the rooster turned out to be a liar against the dog, it turned pail and got ashamed.

The next day, when it ate the bread began to talk.

- Oh liar rooster! You are a liar. You said that the horse would die. Perhaps it died but in another place.

The rooster which was aware of that said:

- Don't worry, tomorrow his mule will die. Then there will be feast for you.

Upon those words, the landowner sold the mule, too. he was saved both from sorrow and loss.

In the third day, the dog said to the rooster:

- Oh master of liars, what happened to your words?

- He immediately sold the mule but tomorrow his slave will catch a merciless disease. When his slave dies he will give you a good feast.

Upon those words the man sold his slave too. He said:

- Thanks to God. I was saved from three troubles to experience. Since I learned the language of the rooster and the dog I saved myself from disadvantages.

Next day, the frustrated dog said:

- Oh nonsensically talking rooster. None of your words turned out to be right. Your lies do not end.

The rooster said:

- I don't lie. Tomorrow, the landowner will die. They will cook too much meal then you can be delighted. Not only you but also all the people of village can be delighted.

The man paid attention to what the rooster said. When he heard that he would die, he began to worry. He suddenly went to the presence of Moses and begged him.

- Oh Moses! Rescue me, save me from that. Prophet Moses said:

- Sell you as you sold the horse, the mule, and the slave and relaxed. So that you got experienced in selling, do it again.

The man said:

- Oh well-mannered prophet! Do not sling up what I have done. Save me.

Prophet Moses said:

- My son! It is too late. What God decides does not change. However, I wish you went to the next world religious.

Just at that moment the man felt sick at his stomach, they brought a cup. Four men took him and carried him to his home. At dawn, prophet Moses prayed for him not to die, without religious, as an unbeliever.

WHAT DOES DOUBLE BLINDNESS MEAN?

Once, there was a blind beggar. While he was begging, he said, "oh people! Pity me, mercy me. I have double blindness, for that reason, pity me two times".

A man said, "I understood your first blindness but I couldn't understand the other. What is it?"

The beggar said: "my voice is bad. It can be regarded as double blindness not to see and to have a bad voice. The people who hear my bad voice while begging are disturbed and get away".

After that his showing his condition and telling the truth provided people to mercy him.

THE OLD MUSICIAN

In Caliph Omer's time, there was a musician who had a very nice voice and a fixture. The people who heard that nice voice became more and more happy. His voice and breath adorned communities and councils.

He was such a musician that the world would be full of happiness thanks to him. Now, no one was giving importance to his voice.

In such times he was begging God:

- Oh my God! Now, I don't have any profit. I am not very weak. You gave me a long life. You have never cut my portion down. Oh my God today I will play for you.

The old musician shouldered the instrument. He began to go towards, Medina graveyard in order to play instrument and shelter God. He said to himself:

- I want the price of instrument, which I will play from God. Forwhy he accepts people who are honest.

He played a long time, he cried and later he made it pillow. He put his head on instrument near the grave and slept.

Sleep carried him away. He left his instrument and playing it. The soul of the musician was walking around in his dream world. He said-I wish, they left me here, they gave me a place here it would be very well. In this dream world, I would travel indefinitely. I would eat a hundred candies.

Meanwhile, prophet Omer fell asleep he couldn't wake up. He said:

- Oh my God! I am not accustomed to such a sleep. That sleep cannot be without any reason. I think it comes from meaning world.

He put his head to the pillow and slept. He saw a dream; in his dream a voice came from God. His soul heard that voice.

The voice said:

- Oh Omer! Save our man from his need. This man is special and respected. Go to the grave to see him. Give him seven hundred dinars, which he needs and desires from treasure. Take that money to him and say "oh man of God, I brought this for you, for now this will meet your need. Spent this and when it finishes come here".

Prophet Omer got ashamed of the majesty of the voice he heard in his dream, jumped and stoop up and prepared to do this work. He took the money under his arms and went to grave.

He began to look for this special man of God. He walked around the grave for a long time. But he could see nobody apart form that old musician. He said to himself:

- That cannot be the special man of God. But he could not find anybody else. Later, he came and stood in front of the musician respectfully. Meanwhile, Prophet Omer took stones in his hand and hit them each other to wake him up without fearing him. The old man woke up, jumped and stood up. He saw Prophet Musa and got surprised. He wanted to go and began to tremble. He said to himself "Oh my God! Help me. How come caliph came near such an old musician like me?"

When Prophet Musa looked at his face, he saw him ashamed and pale. He said:

- Do not be afraid of me. I will announce good news. God praised you so much that Prophet Omer fell in love with your face. Come and sit near me. Here is some gold that you need. Spend it and come here again.

When the old man heard those words, he began to cry.

WHAT DID HE DRINK?

The guard of the quarter came to a place in the midnight. He saw that a "drunk was sleeping near a wall. He asked:

- Hey! What are you doing here? Are you drunk?

The drunken person said:

- I drank what there was in the pitcher.

The guard asked:

- What was in the pitcher?

The drunken said:

- Does it matter what I drank?

The guard said:

- I couldn't understand what you said.

The drunken said:

- A secret thing in the pitcher.

Their conversation went on like this. The guard wanted to understand whether he drank wine or not from the smell of his mouth. He said:

- Come on! Say "ah".

The drunk began to say *HU, HU*

The guard said:

- I tell you to say AH but you say HU

The drunken said:

- I am a cheerful person. I cannot say AH. I think you are sorrowful. Sorrowful people say AH , cheerful people say HU.

The guard said:

- It is none of my business. Come on and stand up. Stop being stubborn; do not pretend to be scholar.

The drunken said:

- Have it your own way, where am I and where are you?

The guard said:

- You are drunk. Just come to the prison with me.

The drunken could not endure and said:

- Oh guard! Leave me have it your own way! What can you take from a nudist? If I could effort to walk, would I fall and stay here? I would go to my own home. If I were clever and found an opportunity, I would guide the people. No one can be harmed by me. Struggle against the people who are drunk without drinking and who exploit people unmercifully.

WHITE HAIRED MAN

An old man whose beard and moustache were white came to a barber in a horror and ordered him to separate the white bristle in his hair and beard and told that he would marry to a new bride.

The barber looked at his hair and beard and understood that it was not possible, so he cut all his hair and beard and put them in front of him.

- I have an urgent work. Excuse me. -Separate white bristles until I come.

DOES GOD HEAR US?

A dervish left his sleep especially in nights and said "Allah" four hundred times and became very happy with that.

In such a night he heard a word which was set to him this word was "oh dervish! You have been saying 'Allah' for such a long time but you have never heard the got to say you 'yes my man'. Until when you will continue that stupidity and waste your time?"

Upon this, dervish became upset. He could not realise that who said that was the Satan. He gave up chanting God. He went bed with that mood and slept. He saw Hizir in his dream. He said: "why did you give up the chant you had been doing?"

Dervish told the situation "I have been chanting to that time but I have never heard the God to say me 'yes my man' even once. I gave up for that reason."

Upon this Hizir said: "your ear doesn't hear God to say you 'yes my man' after chanting but the truth is like that. Is it possible for you to say 'Allah' if he doesn't want." And he relaxed the dervish.

THE BEGGAR AND THE LANDOWNER

A poor person was about to die of hunger. He wanted a piece of bread from a house. The landowner:

- How can you think that there is bread here? Is here a bread furnace?

Upon this the poor man answered:

- So, give me at least some oil.

The landowner said:

- Do you think here is a market?

The poor man said:

- Don't you have even some wheat? Give me at least some meat.

The landowner again found an excuse:

- I think you thought here mill. Do I have such an appearance? Go away from my door. The poor man said:

- Alright, I gave up everything. Please give me a glass of water.

The landowner said:

- Do you think here is a river? How can I find water?

When the man understood that he could get nothing and came across with a mean landowner he tent to urinate by entering his home. Upon this the landowner got angry with the man and asked him why he had done like that.

The man replied:

- You can only urinate in such an empty house

NO BLOCKAGE TO THE THEIF

When a storyteller was telling nice stories to the crowd gathered there, it was time to tell how the tailors steal fabric. Meanwhile, a Turk got angry due to the fact that tailors' secret was revealed. The storyteller told the abuse of tailors extravagantly. Turk became upset by the stories. Later, he could not put up with and asked:

- Oh storyteller! Who is the best tailor in treachery and cheat in your city?

The storyteller answered:

- There is a tailor named Cigeroglu in our city. He is the fastest of all in sleight of hand and theft.

Turk said:

- Let alone the fabric he cannot even steal rope from me.

The storyteller said:

- Do not trust you so much. He deceived the ones much more vigilant than you. You get shocked upon seeing his treacheries.

Turk got angrier and bet saying that:

- That tailor can steal anything neither old nor new from me.

The people around him made him angrier. And he gave whatever he had a security for a loan.

- I pawned my Arabic horse too. If he can steal something from me, let it be yours. If he cannot steal anything from me, I want one more horse with that.

Turk could not sleep because of his sorrow that night. He fought against the vision of thief.

When it was morning, he took silk under his arm. He went to the market of that trickster. After greeting him, he entered the market. The tailor just stood up and returned his bow. He greeted him. He showed great respect to Turk more than necessary. Thus, he won his heard. He had him love himself.

When Turk saw that tailor was saying soft words, Turk threw the silk that he brought in front of the tailor.

- Cut out that cloth a caftan in order to wear in war day which is large below novel and tight above. It should be tight above loins so that it looks nice. It should be large below so that I can move comfortably.

The tailor said:

- Oh dear customer! It is an honour to serve you for me. Your wish is my command.

The tailor later measured the fabric and understood how it would be. Later, by saying soft words he buttonholed Turk. He beguiled Turk with lots of anecdotes and tales. He took the scissors; he was bought cutting the fabric and frequently telling absurd things.

The pledge and pleasantness of the stories the tailor told took the bag of Turk out of his mind. They made him forget everything.

What was silk? What was to bed? What was security? Turk was absorbed in what the tailor told.

When it was Turk's time he said:

- I beg you; teli one more story to laugh. Your words made me comfort.

The trickster tailor told one more thing to laugh. Turk burst out laughing to such extend that he lied down on his back. When inattentive Turk was enjoying, the stories the tailor told, the tailor cut on more piece of fabric and out it into his bosom from the collar of his shire.

Turk said:

- I beg you; tell one more thing to laugh.

This time the tailor told a much more beautiful and much funnier story than the previous ones. He deceived Turk utterly. Turk who bet for horse was now distracted and laughing so much made his eyes close.

The tailor stole one more piece of fabric. Forwhy he found an opportunity while Turk was laughing.

When Turk wanted him to tell something to laugh for the fourth time, the tailor became merciful and decided to seek his theft to the others.

Turk began to beg:

- Tell one thing to laugh.

The reply of the tailor to that demand was a bit satiric:

- Oh man himself is story, until when will you try to listen to stories. There is nothing funnier than your own life. Oh the captive person of laughers! Now leave me. If I tell you one more thin.